SPOKEN

and

UNSPOKEN

MESSAGES

REV. DR. DIANE CROSS

ISBN 978-1-0980-3088-9 (paperback)
ISBN 978-1-0980-3089-6 (digital)

Christian Faith Publishing, Inc.
832 Park Avenue
Meadville, PA 16335
www.christianfaithpublishing.com

Photographed by Aaron Cross
'Aaron Cross as Book Cover Designer', Make-Up and Hair Stylist was done by Marlena C. Rooker

Printed in the United States of America

Endorsements

Dr. Diane Cross shows her dedication to Christ through the many years. She does so by showing up to church every Sunday and teaches kids about the Bible. She teaches kids the importance of the Bible and how much Jesus loves us. She is faithful to her church and bless others in her day-to-day life. Dr. Diane Cross is truly blessed to be a blessing!

—Trelin Thomas (June 26, 2019)

Dr. Diane Cross, a wonderful lady who not only helped me but so many others. She taught me a lot of things. She did one-on-one help to get us to understand her teachings. She gave me lots of knowledge that I use today. She is just a caring, loving, intelligent, very kindhearted women. I appreciate her for teaching me everything.

—Azarian Armstrong

My friend and sister in Christ, Dr. Diane Cross, is a woman that walks in love at all times. The Bible said that because "God is Love," we should always try to be like Him and to represent Him. I have known Dr. Diane for several years, and I have seen her kindness. She is always willing to help and to volunteer wherever she is needed. She has a sincere spirit of excellence. She is a good leader and a good follower. She is devoted in Christian love.

Just as the Bible teaches us to do, she loves her neighbors. Our neighbors are everyone that we come into contact with. Dr. Diane meets no strangers and always has a nice smile for everyone. Love is not selfish.

Dr. Diane will pick you up in her car and take you to the house of God. She welcomes you with a good attitude and a pleasant personality. She is one of God's chosen people. She speaks often and very highly of her family members because she loves them.

This is my opinion and description of my faithful friend, my church member, and my spiritual daughter. That's love and *love never fails*.

—Mother Vashti Thompson

The Bible says love never failed, and that is the character of Dr. Diane Cross. She is always attending events of her children and grandchildren, supporting them by showing how much she cares for them. What a love she has for her family.

She is loving to her church members, helping wherever she can. It does not matter what title she carries, she serves where needed. I'm glad for myself that she has taken time to pray with me, sometimes at 6 a.m., but we got it in! We have had many conversations to support one another, and she has been a real friend to me. I love you, Dr. Diane Cross.

—Evangelist Regina Hill

Dr. Diane Cross has brilliantly written this book on faith and love to help build up any one that have been through any kind of abuse or hurt in their life. She is an excellent teacher, very authentic and honest. By sharing her experiences of what she has gone through in her personal life, she has help so many people. She loves to inspire, edify, and build up others that have those same experience. Her mission in this book is to share with her audience her faith in God and her love of all people. This book is for women, men, and children, and I also recommend counselors to use this book because they would greatly benefit from this book and their clients. This would be a wonderful counseling tool

—Dr. Rowena Horton

Contents

ACKNOWLEDGMENTS

I remember back on one of ministry school assignments, and it was the first time I needed to speak a short message to the class. I had to come out of my fear of speaking in front of others about the Lord. At the same time, I was taking another class lesson at a church, I believe it was on leadership. As I was leaving class, I approached the pastor who was teaching. I told him I was a little scared because I was going to be tested on how I presented myself while giving messages, and I was even going to be timed. I never forgot the lesson I learned from him that day. He told me never to be afraid to speak about the Lord to anybody because it might be your last time to be able to do so.

I do believe in angels which are sent from above in the times of need. But mostly, I believe in the Father, the Son, and the Holy Spirit, which I do give honor, glory, and all praises to our heavenly Father, which is the head of my life, which art in heaven. He is worthy of all.

We must give thanks where honor is due, and I would like to give special honor to all in the pulpit of the churches at hand.

I would like to give thanks to my late husband, who was always trying to make a way, having transportation for me to get back and forth to church.

I thank all ministers who have given me so much over the pulpit in speaking into my life, including all of the Bible studying and teachings that I have attended though phone or in your presence. I thank you for letting God use you in such a way that I really can't explain how much it has helped me through my journey of life. Glory be to God!

Also, to all the mothers, sisters, and brothers of the churches I have attended who have given me a word or two in time of needs.

Thank you to my family and close friends!

A special thank you to Dr. Regina Patrick for many days of prayer and Bible study.

A special thank you goes to Evangelist Regina Hill for the encouraging words you've given me from time to time.

Desmond Weems and Robert Gilmore, thanks for the insights to help me find my way on this journey, and a very special thank you to Regina Cross for such powerful encouraging words to me to continue writing *Spoken and Unspoken Messages*.

To me you all are angels that God has sent in my life. Thank you! Love each of you very deeply.

The Lord's Prayer

Our Father which art in heaven, Hallowed be thine name.

Thy kingdom come. Thy will be done on earth, as it is in heaven.

Give us this day our daily bread.

And forgive us our debts, as we forgive our debtors.

And lead us not into temptation, but deliver us from evil: for thine is the

Kingdom, and the power, and the glory, forever.

Amen! (Matt. 6:9–13, KJV)

Words from the Lord

He was preparing,
Preparing me for you
God has a plan
Can you see how?
He prepared me to help others
Why God? Why Me?
Look where He brought me from
How He prepared me
Learning by experience
Just tell the truth
Don't be Afraid
Can't tell it all
There are dots between the lines
There are lines between the dots
What is your real connection?
Teaching by experience?

APPRECIATION

Thank you to my family and friends who encouraged me to write *Spoken and Unspoken Messages* after hearing a few of my words of messages that had been spoken to them. Thank you for telling me my words will encourage or inspire others just as much as it helped them in the time they needed to hear a word, knowing that God is an on-time God.

Most of all, I give thanks to my Lord Savior. He woke me up one night, telling me to write another book right now and gave me the title right then, saying "Others need to hear from me through your messages." So with obedience, I shall go forth with the instruction of the Lord with my new assignment.

Foreword

Have any of you ever had the blessing of actually having a living guardian angel in your life? Well, I have one. Her name is Dr. Diane Cross. This woman of God is so faithful, honest, and true to anything she puts her mind, body, and soul into. I'm so blessed to have her as a sister, but most of all, a friend.

As we all may know, the most important principle of leadership is integrity. It is better to be honest than to delude others because you are probably deluding yourself too. With that being said, in my heart, I feel my living guardian angel and my messenger, Dr. Diane Cross, has been sent on a special mission.

I have learned there are three aspects of *Faith*: *knowledge*, which is a body of facts or information gained through study and experience; *belief* is trust, faith, or confidence in someone or something; and last is *trust*, which is the belief in the reliability, truth, ability or strength. I have also learned that love plays the biggest part of all. "Love is kind, It does not envy, it does not boast, it is not proud. It does not dishonor others, it is not self-seeking, it is not easily angered, it keeps no record of wrongs" (1 Cor. 13:4–5).

So out of my studying and experiences, I learned a blessed person gives cheerfully because of all that God has given them, and blessings are a part of living a blessed life.

I'm going to share my blessings with you and share her with you. Don't worry, Jesus won't mind. That's sharing faith, love, and integrity where, in the long run, you'll be able to receive peace, love, happiness, and blessings. I pray this book will be a healing and a blessing to you.

Phillip Xavier Terrance Brown Sr.

PRELUDE

To all those reading *Spoken and Unspoken Messages*, I am hoping through faith, hope, and love that you forever let your light shine bright. There are people who needs to hear others' testimonies. With these few, I am hoping that these will help you to guide others in the pathway to our bright and shining light, our Lord and Savior. Psalm 119:105 says, "Thy word is a lamp unto my feet, and a light unto my path."

The Lord has prepared me to be a minister and a distributor of messages, helping others to see how He has prepared you and I with His purpose to finish His plan. "And we know that all things work together for good to them that love God, to them who are called according to his purpose" (Rom. 8:28). Keep praying, have faith, trust in Him, and believing in your relationship with Him.

INTRODUCTION

I wanted to write this book to motivate others by divine influence and to give inspiration to thoughts to be put into action.

> Charity suffereth long and is kind; charity envieth not; charity vaunteth not itself, is not puffed up. (1 Cor. 13:4).

> And now abideth faith, hope, charity, these three; but the greatest of these three is charity. [Love does not brag, arrogant.] (1 Cor. 13:13)

I am quoting these scriptures from the love letter, The Holy Bible, which edified me and in hopes that it will help to build you up even by just you knowing.
Romans 15:4 says,

> For whatsoever things were written for learning that we through patience and comfort of scripture might have hope, not forgetting.

Also Romans 15:2,

> Let every one of us please his neighbour for his good to edification.

Amen! Lord knows my heart. He knows I want to encourage all with the love and teachings that He has stored in me through my life experiences and the encouragements that others have spoken into my heart to share all that I have learned from them. He knows writing is one of my ways that I can edify others, and so I wrote *Spoken and Unspoken Messages*.

I give honor, glory, and all praise to my Lord Savior in Jesus's name. Amen!

PART 1

Faith

The word in itself means to trust, unquestioning belief, and confidence in the testimony of another, particularly God's promise of salvation and eternal life for all who places their trust in Jesus Christ (John 5:24). A gift of God, faith is essential to salvation. (Eph. 2:8) The word also refers to the teaching of Scripture or the faith which was once delivered unto the saints (Jude 3).

Faith Waits Patiently

May 26, 2011

Praise the Lord!
My message is from the book of James 1:2–5,

> (2) My Brethren, count it all joy when ye fall into divers temptations;
> (3) Knowing this, that the trying of your faith worketh patience
> (4) But let patience have her perfect work, that ye may be perfect and entire, wanting nothing.
> (5) If any of you lack wisdom, let him ask of God, that giveth to all men liberally, and upbraideth not; and it shall be given him.

Going through trials and tribulations is a test of our faith. We go through all types of mixed-up natural situations. We all have our work cut out for us. But do we have the patience with belief to go through and ask God for what's in our hearts and wait? In Hebrew 11: 6, it says, "But without faith it is impossible to please him: for he that cometh to God must believe that he is a rewarder of them that diligently seek him." Can we just wait like Abel, Noah, Sarah, Abraham, and others to receive our inheritance, strength, and promises by obeying the Word of God with faith?

Just going through that should have us thinking about self-control over our passions, desires, and habits, such as "I want," "I need," "right now," "I never," "I can't," or "they" or "them." There is a way for us to grow up dealing with ourselves, with others, and all circumstance. "Wherefore seeing we also are compassed about with so great a cloud of witnesses, let us lay aside every weight, and sin which doth so easily beset us, and let us run with patience the race that is set before us" (Heb. 12:1).

At many times, things seem to be set so low in our lives. Our self-esteem gets just so low, and it feels as if we are choking, chained up, and can't get loose. You feel like you just can't put your hands on it. You don't know where it's coming from. Things such as finances to take care of our bills, getting and keeping jobs, transportation, getting to and from destinations and church. Even how we want to serve the Lord may cross our mind.

We have troubles in marriages, troubles with our children, health problems concerning ourselves and loved ones we pray about. But do we pray in *faith* and belief with patience? Most things take time to be answered according to our needs and the will of God, Amen. Do you have *faith* to wait patiently for things to work out in God's time, not our own?

When it seems too long of a wait, we can be tempted to do or say things that are not of God, but the devil's. Sometimes God has better things in store for us if we only just have *faith* and wait patiently with belief.

It could be a new car, a new home, a new position on the job, or a new lifestyle in general—a change in you. It could be just teaching you how to get closer to God Himself. We have to remember we go through trials and tribulations to get where God wants us to be, Amen.

Faith waits patiently for the coming of the Lord, and with love. I have learned that no matter what the situation seems, good or bad, God causes all things to work together for the good, and even bad things will turn to be good.

We must go through trials and tribulations, such as emotions of forgiveness and loving one another. We can't forget our wants and needs or even health issues to get ourselves cured and repaired to receive wisdom and blessings that the Lord has for us. "And not only so, but we glory in tribulations also: knowing that tribulation worketh patience; And patience, experience; and experience, hope" (Rom. 5:3–4). Going through affliction and hoping for things builds our relationship and faith within God.

I trust God in all things. I have a praise in my heart at all times for the Lord. (How about you?) I have learned trials come and go, coming out of one thing into another. It just seems never-ending. Talking faith is not enough, we must believe and trust with confidence that everything is going to be all right. We shouldn't walk with a cloud over our heads, having low self-esteem. Don't you know faith can meet circumstance head on? *Faith* gets you to be a doer, not just a hearer. Get out and be a witness!

I know at times it may seem there is no joy and peace. Think of the goodness the Lord brought you from. Putting food on your table, clothes and shoes on your back and feet, keeping a roof over your head even when you're going through foreclosure and eviction. God hasn't thrown you out, He has only given you more love of grace and mercy. Just hold on (wait!) with faith and believe with patience, knowing He is an on-time God and supplied all your needs. Lift yourself up in a new clean spiritual heart with faith. Let your light shine, and tell others how good the Lord has been to you.

Faith controls the tongue; it keeps it in check, it humbles you, and it helps you to resist the devil. You will even complain less, especially if you don't have things all twisted up. Just listen for His voice, He will tell you if you're right or wrong, which way to turn, or just be still and listen. He is a righteous God.

Jesus is the author and the finisher of our *faith*. Don't forget Jehovah is our healer of joy and peace. Amen. Keep in mind, have *faith*, hope, and love always. In order to build *faith*, we should obey the Word just as *faith* obeys the Word.

The Word says ask God! Should we stop asking with *faith* for things because it's taking too long? I say put your *faith* to work. If you haven't given Him a try, try Him! *Faith* waits patiently with belief. How strong is your *faith* to wait patiently with belief and a praise in your heart at all times? Thank God for teaching *faith* and patience with belief through trials and tribulations. Amen! Give God your highest praise. Hallelujah!

Can You Believe You Can Believe?

Glory be to God. All things are possible. I am here to tell you that yes, you can believe because believing is a choice. It means to accept or trust fully. You may or may not know belief or trust is in Christ. It is necessary for salvation and necessary to righteousness. You can believe by using your *faith* and trust, having confidence.

In Matthew 10:17–21, Christ warned we may be deceived and be unworthy of trust, but we may place all our trust and confidence in Him. God gave you a measure of faith. We all need to exercise our *faith*.

It's satan's power and evil heart and self-glorification and pride that cause disbelief. He is the enemy who comes to steal from us.

There is *faith* in you. "*Faith* cometh by hearing and the hearing by the Word of God" (Rom. 10:17). There is a story in the Bible of a woman with the issues of blood. This is in the book of Matthew. It is telling us that a woman heard about all the work Jesus has been doing. From then on, she started believing in all the sayings he had been teaching for others. She started believing that if only she could just touch the hem of His garment, she would be healed. So she pressed her way to touch the hem and she was healed.

Today, we can still touch the hem of His garment. All we have to do is believe, knowing that believing is having trust, faith, and confidence in Jesus, just like the women with the issues of blood.

Don't forget there is a saying that states "What you don't use, you can lose it." So be confident in using your trust and *faith* in Jesus. Amen!

We all should be like palm trees. When a storm comes, we should be able to tolerate it, ride it out, just stand firm when it comes through. It's telling us we should ask with faith, not wavering (James

1:6). Because when wavering, it's like at sea of waves driven with wind and tossed.

That's like saying "I believe" or "I think I believe." Which way are you believing? You know believing is a decision and *faith* is what you believe.

Mark 11:22–24 (KJV) says,

> (22) Have *faith* in God.
>
> (23) for verily I say unto you, That whosoever shall say unto this mountain, be thou removed, and be thou cast into the sea; and shall not doubt in his heart, but shall believe that those things which he saith shall come to pass; he shall have whatsoever he saith.
>
> (24) Therefore, I say unto you, What things so ever ye desire, when ye pray, believe that ye receive them, and ye shall have them.

God took an oath to speak the truth and to keep His promise. You can read in Hebrews 6:16–18.

There are two unchangeable things in which it's impossible for God to lie. The first is that we have a strong comfort that is being protected or sheltered, keeping us from feeling sad. The other is hope, which anchors our soul and keeps it from drifting.

Mountains are issues. When you believe is when you can receive. The mountain could be your health issues, money issues, or family issues. But before we receive, we all have to pray, praise, and believe before the healing takes place. We shouldn't act like our illness is still there. We need to get in line with our mouth and say it, call it, and talk it. We must demand it by saying "I'm healed!" You have the authority and the power. You have the Word. Stand on the Word, stand on the blood, speak it, and have faith (*believe*). Glorify God, say you're blessed. When you're feeling sick, say you're healed. Lay hands on the sick, lay hand on yourself. God said that by His stripes, you're healed.

I'm a cancer survivor. Amen! As I was going through, I've learned to read healing scriptures. There is one I read over and over again because I felt it was pertaining to me and my condition. I was afraid and it told me not to fear. The Lord will hold my hand and help me, and I really did believe He would, especially when I was going though chemo. This scripture talks about how having a new sharp instrument that thrashes the mountain (issue) and beats them small and fan them, and the wind shall carry them away. At the end, it says, "And shall rejoice in the Lord. And glory in the Holy One" (Isa. 41:13–16). This is the main scripture I read daily with belief, saying, "I am healed by His stripes!"

I also wouldn't listen or hear any negative talk about my condition, and I was praying all the time. The tumor was beaten small enough for the surgery and was carried away. I'm still praising and glorifying the Lord to this day and forever. Amen! You can read scriptures pertaining to your situations and put them down inside of you with belief.

If you feel you're poor, stop saying it. Say "I'm rich." Speak out on your job situation, your home situations, or whatever other mountains you have. You just need to believe. It might seem like a struggle at these times but don't fight it. Just believe that God does the fighting for you.

Stand on the Word and stay focused. The devil seeks whom he can take in. We all have heard the saying "What you see is what you get." The enemy is always playing with our minds. I encourage you to read scriptures that pertain to your situations. The more you read, the more you will say them and truly believe the motivation within them.

We all have to be in the right mindset for believing and speaking things so you must confess. Your mind is your gateway. You have to stand guard over your gate, and you must be the gatekeeper. Lock your mind at night to keep the enemy out. Take power over your mind because the stronghold is in the mind. Control your thoughts.

When you believe, you can begin seeing things happening. Can you believe you can believe? Now in the spirit God gave as healing power, but we will have to believe for it to come in the nature. Amen!

Praying with Belief

*M*ay 31, 2009

My message from the book of 1 John 5:13–15,

> (13) These things have written unto you
> that believe on the name of the son of God; that
> ye may know that ye have eternal life, and that ye
> may believe on the name of the Son of God.
>
> (14) And this is the confidence that we have
> in him, that if we ask any thing according to his
> will, he hearth us;
>
> (15) and if we know that he hears us, what-
> soever we ask, we know that we have the peti-
> tions that we desired of him.

Verse 13 reminds me when we pray. It is breath to the spirit. Not praying is the same as having a dead body that doesn't breathe. God is the best fresh air for our spirit. When we have conversation with God, our spirit is breathing, it is alive. God is a spirit there for eternal life (John 4:24).

Most of us worry about everyday situations such as are home, jobs, children, health, even our church homes. This is normal. It's the flesh of us. We try to keep a roof over our head and food on our table. We have dreams for our children, although most of the times, they have different dreams than us. But we continue to pray for our family's protection each and every day and night.

These are some of the things we pray and ask for according to His will. Also, we wonder if we're going to have a job to help us to make it day after day, especially with the way economy is these days. Don't forget our physical well-being, some looking for a miracle for different diseases: leg injury, back surgery, kidney, heart transplant, you name it, or just having health insurance. Not forgetting some of our church homes, wondering if we will have a place to fellowship together and worship to praise the Lord because of finance these days.

Just praying about all things isn't enough. Not by just saying a few words and that is it. We should have faith in God that our situation will change as we pray. It says in Hebrew 11:6, "But without faith it is impossible to please him: for that cometh to God must believe that he is, and that he is a rewarder of them that seek him."

There have been times I had to put all my faith with God, for instance where I only had one day to save my home according to men, (but only God), and it was saved. More than once in my lifetime, I have set the table anyway didn't know where the meal is coming from and there was food on my table. (Praise the Lord). Each day praying for protection over my children or other family members. Praying when my children get sick day or night. Praying with faith and belief for other mothers, fathers, their brothers, sisters, cousins, or just a friend, not forgetting the sick, those who are hungry and the homeless. Praying over jobs for others and myself, wanting help to make it day after day. Not knowing how some bills will be paid time after time. Hoping for my church home. But the Word says in Matthew 21:22, "And all things whatsoever ye shall ask in pray. Believing, ye shall receive."

Are you praying with belief? I am here to tell you that I am one of those who have prayed about each of these circumstances. Have there been times when things seem to you unbearable when weakness sets in? When it seems you can't pray anymore, words just wouldn't come out. Have you been this way? I have learned to have faith and believe in the power that is given from up high (Luke 24:49). God causes all things to work together for the good. Even bad things will turn to good. I learned through my life experience that He was always there. I just couldn't see.

I am a walking miracle form a heart attack seven years ago. I was transferred from three different hospitals because one or the other didn't do this or that procedure concerning my heart. I laid on the operating table wide awake through the whole surgery, watching and listening while the doctors and their interns make a couple of mistakes to be corrected right then and there. I couldn't do anything but talk to the Lord who is the real doctor, my healer.

We had an accident last year, involving my husband, sister-in-law, and myself. We were hit by an eighteen-wheeler truck and rolled over at least ten times, I was told. I was watching from the side of the freeway, and the rescuers came running with body bags, looking for survivors. My family could have been making funeral arrangements at that time but instead saw a miracle.

The main thing I really remember is calling on Jesus when the car was flipping and flopping to land. I know Jesus heard my cry because I am here to speak to you today. Praise the Lord. Hallelujah. Thank you, Jesus. I am a walking miracle.

Thinking back on my life, I am a true believer when I pray. This one incident seemed like a bad thing but turned out to be good. It's a good thing because I wouldn't have known about my cancer if it hadn't been for the accident taking place, thinking it's another injury taking place on my body instead of a disease called cancer.

Just hearing doctors saying we can do something and not saying hearing we can't do anything. Lead me to believe, He is an on-time God. I am one who have been praying for a miracle for my health, having confidence with true belief that I'm healed because the Word says I am healed by His stripes. Looking back at all that the Lord has done and is doing for you and me, do you have confidence? I ask you, are you a true believer when you pray?

Saints, we need to take some things to the altar and leave them and remember that we go through trials and tribulations to get were God wants us to be. At these times, it may seem that there is no joy and peace. Don't forget we have Jehovah, our healer of joy and peace. God Almighty provided all with His almighty power. "For the Word of God is quick and powerful and sharper than any two-edged sword, piercing even to the dividing asunder of soul and spirit and of the joints and marrow and is discerned of thoughts and intents of the heart" (Heb. 4:12).

I say to all, especially on our intercessory prayers, we must be true believer when praying. We must be on one accord to His will. He hears us.

I leave this thought with you: The power of Faith and true belief will work no matter where you're on earth though prayer. Don't be selfish of power. Use the knowledge of knowing when you need help to pray, giving thanks to God for what He has done, is doing, and yet to do for you. Have patience on waiting on time, God's time is not your own. Intercession is a gift of love to help someone when they are weak to pray for themselves. Remember faith, hope, and love. The greatest is love.

I ask again, are you praying with belief? True belief? I leave with one more scripture to give to you: "I will therefore that men pray everywhere, lifting up holy hands without wrath and doubting" (1 Tim. 2:8). Amen!

When It's Not Easy

September 10, 2017

My message is from the book of Isaiah 40:31. I am going to read the King James Version. The King James Version says, "But they that wait upon the Lord shall renew their strength; they shall mount up with wings as eagles; they shall run and not be weary and they shall walk, and not faint." Amen.

How many of you know that the word *wait* means to remain until something expected happens and to be ready? When things are expected, we should be prepared to use or act on them immediately. We all know the Lord has the authority. In other words, He has the power or right to command.

Before going any farther about speaking on *When It Is Not Easy*, I would like first to tell you a little bit about the eagle. Eagle conveys the powers and messages of the spirit. It is man's connection to dive because it flies higher than all other birds. The symbolic meaning of the wings of an eagle represents our faith.

Eagle has appeared, and it bestows freedom and courage to look ahead. The eagle flies on the wind thermals. The symbolic meaning of the wind is the Holy Spirit. The thermal is the rising air. Eagle symbolizes pure spirit. It is the symbol of honesty and truthful principle. It does not mix with other birds. It enjoys flying on high altitude. It will never surrender to the size or strength of its prey.

The eagle spends a lot of time waiting. When they feel a thermal, they stay in the thermal to gain strength. The eagle is a prey. It hunts. It sizes up its food. An eagle doesn't flap its wings, it soars. By flapping, it uses up too much energy and can easily die. At the same time, it sits and waits, watching or studying on the prey. If it sits on its perch too long, it could die from not eating and keeping its strength.

We have to learn how to walk and fly on the power of the Holy Spirit in our lives, just like the eagle. The eagle soars as high as the wind goes, which is like having faith and belief in God. We are the eagle in our Christian walk.

Can you see why it doesn't mix with other birds? It feels courage and freedom, just looking ahead. That's trusting the Holy Spirit. It doesn't flap its wings to get higher like us humans. Most of us humans are lost and all mixed up without the guidance of the Holy Spirit. If we don't watch out, we would be the victim being attacked by an enemy, swindled, or even ridiculed by a hostile person or disease.

We all go through trials and tribulations, which is a test, and it is not easy because most tests are not made to be easy. We go through all types of mixed up natural situations. We all have our work cut out for us, but do we have the patience and belief like the eagle? There is a season and a time to every purpose here on earth. We need to always be sensitive to the leading of the Holy Spirit, and that is to go to and ask God what's in our hearts and wait, then we will also know if it is our season.

In the Bible, Hebrews 11:6 says, "But without faith it is impossible to please him: for he that cometh to God must believe that He is a rewarder of them that diligently seek him." That means to act but do it carefully and work hard. When it is not easy, we must do our part. It does take hard work, with belief and faith, that we can do whatever it is that needs to be done. After you do the hard part, you will see things come easier.

Sometimes we must wait and not be in such a rush. It might not be the time to do the things that you are hoping for. God isn't going to tell you or show you anything new until you do what he already told you to do. So do what you need to do. Take care of it.

Sometimes when things that you hope for didn't happen, it's because of what you didn't do. God uses foolish things to reward the wise. When God does things, He does it well, and He is a rewarder. God waits on you to get involved. It's not until you do the hard that it becomes easy. Faith without work is dead.

Can we just wait like Abel, Noah, Sarah, Abraham, and others to receive our inheritance, strength, and promises by obeying the Word of God in faith? Look at Abel. His works were called the righteous, and his sacrifices were commanded as a testimony of faith. We have Noah, the chosen one, to preserve life on the earth by building an ark to escape the great flood. He found grace with the Lord. Then we have Sarah who needed strength to conceive, but in order to do so, she had to have faith. And let's not forget Abraham. His faith didn't waver on all the things God had promised to him.

It isn't easy going through, but when we are going through something, it should have us thinking about self-control over our passion, desires, and habits, such as "I want," "I need," "right now," "I never," "I can't," or "they," or "them." When it is not easy, these are some of the areas we feel we are being attacked.

Have you ever heard of the old saying action speaks louder than words? Well, in these areas, we must be careful. Our self-control is really one that stands out to me. The way we treat people or talk to people could make a big difference later on in your life, such as blaming others without looking at yourself first. We want to be treated a certain way in our life, so we need to be careful in these areas. We need patience and faith. Using our action when using the right approach, it could cause easiness later down the line in our life.

There may be someone watching your actions that the Lord may be using to give you a favor or blessing and helping you right then or later. Be careful with your words and the actions that you take, he also uses unsaved people to help you do His will. You could be making things harder for yourself than necessary.

When going to God in are asking, we might say, "Lord, please give me the strength to go through. It's like we need to be renewed and have a fresh start, we need a change in our daily living we even feel we our being attack. But when we ask, do we have the patience to wait on the Lord to receive our renewed strength? We feel at times that we need to be revived. Needing a fresh start, we ask for strength, for our health to be restored, or just help us to return to our normal self. We feel so weak and weary at times that we feel like we can't go on. Even the weight of negative news becomes overwhelming. Do we really have the patience to wait and not feel faint?

God does things that man can't do. We need to walk in love and in confidence. Love never fails. Why not follow the positive? You just need to trust Him. Keep building yourself up and stay in the Word. Have a relationship with God and be willing to hear and respond to His leading. Peter took his eyes off of Jesus and began looking at the wind, the waves, and the storm, then he began to sink. Faith requires us to be led by the spirit. When times are good, we may stray away from God. Don't be a sometimey person with God.

Some Christians gradually start to decline spiritually then find themselves in trouble and wonder what happened. They start living for the flesh and not the spirit. This is called in the Old Testament as *backsliding*, which is being disloyal and unfaithful. Backsliding is like a sickness. It's a secret infection of sin, which leads to loss of spiritual appetite. People gradually decline and if you do not take care of it, it will lead to a slow death.

God heals our backsliding if we honestly accept His diagnosis and humbly return to Him. Give Him an honest heart, and let Him have His way in your life.

We all know that when we know better, we should do better. The Word of God is true. God alone is the source of true wisdom. Wisdom is the principal thing. Wisdom is there when we seek God. So if any of you lack wisdom, ask God. Remember this: Jesus went through everything, and the devil is out to kill, steal, and destroy. Also remember, When it is not easy: While praying about our issues. God knows the purposes before the plan. He doesn't respond to begging, He responses to believing with confidence. Jesus says, "Ask, it will be given to you. Whatever you ask in my name I will do it" (John 14:13–14).

Besides having strength, you should be mount up with wings like eagles. We all have our ups and down, our good and bad times. Stop feeling like you're the only one going through something, there is more than one eagle.

We, as people, sometimes have to encourage ourselves, have hope, be confident, and feel victorious. There is a way for us to rise up and grow up when dealing with ourselves, with others, and in all circumstance. In Hebrews 12:1, it says, "Wherefore seeing we also are compassed about with so great a cloud of witness, let us lay aside every weight, and sin which doth so easily beset us, and let us run with patience the race that is set before us."

You probably never thought that seeing, hearing, smelling, touching and tasting could lead you from faith. Fear is another thing; it's a tool satan uses to destroy your life. It keeps you out of faith in God. God uses things such as what we see and hear to help us make the right decision. But do we pay attention?

There are three types of faith, these are: no faith, little faith, and great faith. The great faith is the one that acts on God's Word alone.

Compassion is an attitude of mercy and forgiveness. It is another word for mercy. God's mercies are abundant and fresh every morning.

Speaking of weight, did you know unforgiveness can weigh you down? Forgiveness surrounds us. I know it is hard to forgive others at times. In these areas of our life which is in our emotion, health, and spiritual. They causes more hard working effort for you to work at. It will have you working harder and harder when it's not easy to forgive.

We can get emotionally sick with unforgiveness. We might toss and turn at night, not sleeping well. We don't have the strength at times when we don't get enough rest. People at times can't forgive themselves. Forgiveness and letting go can lead you down the path of healing and peace. Don't say you forgive someone when you don't; it won't make you feel better. With time, you may find it in your heart to forgive. Learn to forgive yourself, not just others.

When Jesus was on the cross, He asked forgiveness for us and it was given. Receive God's forgiveness for yourselves first because we all have missed the mark with God. We all aren't perfect, but we all want to be Christlike. Amen! If we are not careful, we can cause someone to drift away from God, and it can cost you your relationship with God.

There are times we feel like a yoke is around our neck. It makes us feel like we are choking, chain up, can't get lose. It has our self esteem so low in our life. We don't know where our finances coming from to take care of our bills, how we going to get and keep a job. We sometimes don't have transportation getting to and fro places. These are the things that keeps us so low when we just don't know how.

Some people who don't really cry or weep over anything usually cry over money problems, and that's when joy leaves. In Isaiah 14:3, it's says, "A man's pride shall bring him low: but honor shall uphold the humble spirit." Amen.

Sometimes we think about how we wants to serve the Lord. Some have trouble in marriages, our children, health problems concerning ourselves and loved ones, we pray about them all.

We can start off successful in our life. Sometimes things can get harder for us as we go through life and it could get a little messy on the way through. We do have problems with children and others. You can't change them, but God knows how to get to them. If we want the blessing of God to flow in our lives, stop complaining and criticizing and start praying and giving thanks. Cast the cares to the Lord. The attitudes of our hearts are important to God. The battle is the Lord's, it's not yours. If you don't turn it over to the Lord, you could be fighting fear and stress, which is part of your health.

We all know *up* means "higher." It could be a cause of a rise or to restore power and favor. We have proper support by having the power that was given to us by the Power. We need to learn how to use it. Here is one sorts for you.

I know most of you have heard that death and life is in the power of the tongue, but you must be careful the way you use such power. Not just that power but any reaction you take. Your fasting and praying needs to be done with the right attitude, then all needs would be met. Isaiah 58:3–9 tells us healing would be theirs, and righteousness would open doors for them, and God's glory would protect them from their enemies. God will answer our prayers when we have the right attitude in our hearts.

When it is not easy, we feel like we are being dismantled or just being taken apart in all these areas of life troubles. But in all these areas, we must rise up. We have the authority, the power to rise up like an eagle.

Eagles are large birds that prey. They are hunters and also have sharp vision and powerful wings. The wings itself is to provide a way to pass through or go over. That is some kind of power to have. Amen! But do we have the patience like the eagle when it hunts? It uses its sharp vision, and it moves fast and it improvises to make do with whatever is at hand.

The eagle studies its prey. It sizes them up, and it doesn't waste its strength. It waits while preparing to use what it has learned at the right time, and that is in God's time the Holy Spirit. Amen.

Feed yourself, stay focused in the Word. Don't just sit on it, use it. Don't die not using what you learned with the guidance of the Holy Spirit.

You need to discipline your mind to remain focused so the enemy doesn't defeat you. Just like now, sitting in church, the enemy could be distracting your mind, causing you to miss the Word of God that will change your life. Do you just sit there and do nothing? Eagles study on the animals they're waiting for. It watches then move, but one thing they do, they use what is at hand. Again, do you just sit there and just be a hearer and not be a doer, putting hard work in your action.

Just like your marriage, it takes work. Who said it was easy? I have been with my husband almost fifty years, and it wasn't easy and still isn't. It takes work. People ask me what I feel or what helped my marriage work. I always say communication, forgiveness, and love. It takes work raising your children, feeding them, dressing them, getting them the best education as possible, keeping their health and your health in check and do what the doctors tell you, doing exercises, eating the right food, taking medicines, it takes work. Laziness will cause you to be broke too. Work on these things, and have faith to receive your blessing.

When doing all these things, we need to communicate with the Lord. We ask Him for forgiveness all the time, and the Bible says to forgive but how many times? Seventy times seventy, and our first commandment is love. It takes all these things together for families or marriages to work out. We are in the Lord's family, and He is our Father.

Most things take time to be answered according to our needs and the will of God. Amen. I ask you, do you have patience to wait with faith and believe for things to work out in God's time and not your own? The will of God is our greatest security. Knowing that the future is secure in the Lord is encouragement. We need to find the will of God.

Even in our lives here on earth, it takes time to do or get things done, especially when going to your parents or being a parent. At times, we just don't have the money or other means at hand. We have to wait. Majority of time, we wait until the time is better for us to be able to do them.

Why should we wait for blessings when God can give it now? He washes and cleanses us. He sets us apart for Himself and blesses us in our houses with His presents. In this verse of Isaiah 40:31, it says, "They shall run and not be weary, if they wait on the Lord."

We all need to set aside a day of rest just like God did. Rest and work must be balanced. God may not take away the pain in your heart, such as losing a loved one, but He can balance it with His joy. Man and God must work together to produce.

When it seems to long of a wait, we sometimes get double-minded like the waves of the sea. We analyze things too much. Then we become tempted to do or say things that isn't of God but the devil's. When we feel like we are suffering, that is the time when happy memories get erased, and the sad memories step in place. Remember that God's mercy helps encourage us in this type of trial.

Take control of your thoughts daily so you can be free as the eagle. Having faith in God brings victory, not the faith in man. We are in the world but not of the world. So we all need a different mindset to know how to handle things of this life because we can become what we think about in our minds. Our fleshly desires must die. When we are thinking the same way as the world, we are conforming and not transforming.

Just a small testimony here where I got a little wisdom from some mothers from the church I used to attended. I rented our home out, and the renter destroyed the home so bad it was unbelievable. I didn't want to tell my husband about the house, and I didn't for a long time because of the hard work he had put into it. It was one of the times I could have went to jail for. I went to church still very upset. The mothers prayed for me and told me that when I meet up with the lady about the house, don't fuss and rise sand. I did do what they asked me to do. All I could do was ask the lady why and just cry. She told me right off that if I had come to her cursing and fighting, she would have walked away and done nothing, I founded out some information before I met up with her. I couldn't even sue her by law. But by the grace of God, she promised that she would put the house together the way it was. She kept her promise. Look how God works. This is testimony on how things could have been said or a foolish action that could have taken place.

It seemed to me like it was going to take a long time to put the house together again. The finances just seemed to not be there but look at God. That wasn't easy. It was rough to hold back in telling her a thing or two and beating her down. I probably would've went to jail. It would've probably costed me more than what I've bargained for.

In Proverbs, it says, "Be not wise in thine own eyes: fear the Lord and depart from evil." Look at how God rewarded me by making it easy for me, by giving me wisdom, and I received it from the mothers of the church. Amen!

Sometimes God have better things in store for us if we just wait patiently. It could be a new car, a new home, and new position on the job, or a new lifestyle. How about a renewal in you? It could be just teaching you how to get closer to God Himself.

When it is not easy, we need to remember that we go through trials and tribulations to get where God wants us to be. Amen.

Faith waits patiently for the coming of the Lord, and with love. I have learned that no matter what the situation seems to be, good or bad, God causes all things to work together for the good that even bad things will turn out to be good.

Another area of life to think about is when you are faithful to your calling. Your ministry will not be easy whenever you share the Word with people, expect to be tested, going through trials and tribulations. Men may shut up God's servant, but they can't shut out

God's Word. The Word comes to you no matter where you are if your heart is open to the Lord (2 Tim. 2:9).

Obedience must come from devotion within us and not depending on the circumstances around us. Serving God is a blessing and a privilege, but it is also a difficult task, and it gets more and more difficult. Preaching to others that costs nothing will accomplish you nothing. If we rush to our destiny without proper preparations or at the wrong time, it can destroy us. But if we go to our destiny at God's appointed time, we will be fully equipped to handle whatever situation.

We must go through trials and tribulations, such as emotions of forgiveness and loving one another, not forgetting our wants and needs or health issues. We need to get ourselves cured and repaired to receive wisdom and blessings that the Lord has for us.

"Not only so, but glory in tribulations also: knowing that tribulations worketh patience; And patience, experience; and experience, hope" (Rom. 5:3–4). Going through afflictions and hoping for things also build our relationship and faith with God.

We should trust God in all things. I have a praise in my heart at all times for the Lord. How about You? I have learned that trails come and go. After one thing comes another, and it doesn't seem to end. Talking faith is not enough, we must believe and trust with confidence that everything is going to be all right. We shouldn't walk with a cloud over our heads and have low self-esteem. Don't you know faith can meet circumstances head on? Faith gets you to be a doer, not just a hearer. Get out and be a witness. I know at times it seems there is no joy and peace, but tell the goodness of the Lord and what He has done for you. Think about all of the goodness the Lord has brought you: putting food on your table, clothes and shoes on your back and feet, keeping a roof over your head even when you're going though foreclosures and eviction. God hasn't thrown you out. He has only given you more love and grace and mercy. Just hold on. Wait with faith and patient, knowing that He is an on-time God and supplies all your needs.

When it is not easy, remember that God wants to do big favors in our life. He wants us to have a bountiful life. It is His grace. All

God needs is your faith. He is your helper. He will never leave you or forsake you. He is the same yesterday, today, and forever. Don't dwell on what you don't have or what you have lost because that isn't confidence in God. Praise Him, be grateful. God gives back when we praise Him.

When you are having an experience of feeling down, it is just temporary. Don't be anxious, ask for things humbly. God gives double for your troubles.

Faith creates blessings. He even gave us power to create our life with our mouth. In the beginning, God created the heaven and the earth. God said let there be light He even spoke blessings. We have the authority of all things in the name of Jesus. We have the power to speak blessings over ourselves, and we have the responsibility for our lives. Why not use that power?

I feel like we shouldn't complain about our situation and shouldn't say things, such as when God see it, or using the word if, when, I can't, or it's not easy. Don't let the devil put negative thoughts in you. That's giving him the credit. Remember,

> His wings you shall take refuge; his truth
> shall be your shield and buckler. (Ps. 91:4)

> Only with your eyes shall you look and see
> the reward of the wicked. (Ps. 91:8)

Trust in God's protection over you and your family. Activate your blessing. Receive it. Claim it. Create faith using words like "I am blessed," "I am loved", or "I am highly favored."

So again, one more time, when you feel weak and it is not easy, leave yourself up in a new clean spiritual heart and trust in the power of God, and you can be like an eagle or a runner with easiness, and freely and have patience because in emergencies of life, God helps you soar. In the daily routine of life, He will help you patiently walk with peace and not faint. Amen.

Be blessed, everyone. Let's give God praise! Hallelujah!

It's God's Time, Not Yours

God is a good God. God is a God of blessing. His mercy is new every day. Amen!

I give praise to our Lord Savior and all of you. There is no lack or limits with God. Don't you know we are heirs of God, and we are entitled to everything? In 2 Thessalonians 5:24, it says, "Faithfull is he that calleth you unto also will do it." God sets open doors. There is no lack in God and no limits with God. God has a vision for you. All God needs is your faith. He is your helper. He will never leave you, nor forsake you. Remember that Jesus Christ is the same yester-day, today, and forever. Amen!

God wants to do big things in our life. He wants us to have a boun-tiful life. It is His grace. It is His call, not yours. It is the things that make you uncomfortable that stops your bountiful life. It will limit your life. The very thing you are brushing off could be the thing God was sending you. God sends opportunities. He wants to do new things for you other than what you are doing now. We must recognize the season. Ask God if this is it, but be ready to come out of your comfort zone. Coming out of your comfort zone, you have to pay a price. Step out, stop calling your shots and holding back. Stop saying I can't do this or that. Pay attention to people in your surroundings, recognize. It's God's call, not yours.

You know some of us feel we are at a lost, and we just don't feel we have anything left. I am here to tell you the Holy Spirit can work with what you have left. He can do miracles. Think about the little boy with the two fish and bread. How about the woman with the oil? Both had little but became much. Amen! And let us not forget how Jesus turned water into wine. Amen!

Have you ever tried writing down a list of your leftovers? Because you really don't have a list of losses. Do you have clothes on your back, shoes on your feet, roof over your head, food on your table? You might have a small paycheck, but it is better than nothing at all. You might have lost a mother or a father, but you still got one or the other. Praise Him. Be thankful and grateful for what you have left. Have an attitude daily on what you have left. Just look at the list, and you will realize that you have more than what you thought you had. Receive your bountiful life. Don't dwell on your losses for when you do, that's not having confidence in God. We should check our attitudes, not forgetting that our body is the temple of the Holy Spirit, and there is no testimony without a test.

I suggest that you read 1 Corinthians 2:9–16, but I do want to read part of verse 10, which reads:

> For the Spirit searcheth all things, yea the deep things of God.

I am now going to read verse 14, which reads:

> But natural man receiveth not things of the Spirit of God: for they are foolishness unto Him: neither can he know them, because they are spiritually discerned.

Be godly. Serve others with gladness and with the right spirit.

Praise Him. Be grateful. God gives back when we praise. The feeling that you have of losing someone or something is just a temporary thing. Again do not forget God remains the same. So remain in praise even in all your trials and tribulations.

You know the enemy satan comes to kill, steal, and destroy, and he is a liar. So don't blame Jehovah, God, because he didn't do it. He is a good God. God is God. He is not mad or angry.

Jesus prayed we would understand the things we go through and that it shall pass, such as our health, money, home, job, dreams, and other situations.

Stay in praise. Have gratitude and be grateful. Stay in peace; peace is a blessing. God is a God of blessing. Serve the Lord, you and your family. If God isn't in your home, you don't have peace.

God is God of blessing, full of joy. You will feel and hear His presence, but when you drift away from God, you won't hear His voice.

Trust in God. God gives double for your troubles. His mercy is new every day. Be careful and don't let things slip. Life is too short, repent.

When you are not in agreement with any situation, pray, speak to God. Take authority. The power is in the mouth. Speak to that mountain. With God, all is possible. Walk in love with people. Don't be mad with people you can call things to be not as they're use your power. Humble yourself and take any situation to the Lord. Your problems about your job even your problems at home. Put things in God's hands. Invite Him into your situations. Don't wait on things to happen or take place. You can't always get people to agree with you.

There is a time to stand firm, pray, and fast. There is a time to proceed because God said it. Negative people will say no, this isn't the right time. Some people fear they're not ready instead of walking in God's time. Don't you know God is an on-time God? Remember, it's God's call, not yours. So know if you think you have the provision, such as money or other means for a vision, by throwing your weight around, that is not of God. God's vision is bigger. God has a vision to stretch you even bigger. All God needs is your faith.

It is time to be about your Father's business. This is the season. You don't have to wait on other people's approval. Sometimes you can't tell people your vision. People just can't see what you see when you are looking through God's eyes. They will try to talk you out of it. Just be willing. Believe in God. You don't have to have money or the people you think you should have. Stop excepting help from people who cannot help themselves. God sends people to help you.

Don't be scared to try what God has given you to do. Quit sitting, spend time with God, read scriptures, get prayed up, be wise, be obedient, confess over what you want, talk to God before talking to others, especially your children or your spouse, then things will come to you, such as money, people, and things you would need.

God doesn't want to divide your house. Pray for others when they are in a disagreement with you. You are your energy for stress and frustration. Get yourself healed. Get your own life straightened out. God came to give you a bountiful life. Thank God for everything and walk in faith because that's all He really needs. Remember, it's His call, not yours. Amen!

COMPASSIONATE SAVIOR

2014

Giving honor to all of you.

Coming from the book of Exodus, I will be speaking about Pharaoh's daughter who is known by the given name from the Jewish Rabbis in the Midrash as Bit-Yah which means "the daughter of the Lord." She is known as the adoptive mother of Moses, the prophet and lawgiver, which is legal set of giving statues of a family member to raise as one's own child.

Bit-Yah was very powerful even at the age of six because of her ties to royalty. She rescued Moses as an infant out of the Niles with compassion. Bit-Yah had an attitude of mercy and forgiveness like our compassion Jesus Christ our Savior. She realized he was a Hebrew child. Her servant or handmaids were trying to talk her out of keeping the baby. She didn't listen to them. This is known as a miraculous deliverance.

Bit-Yah had help from his real mother even paid her to nurse him. Pharaoh's daughter named him Moses, loved him, and raised him as her own son. This gave her the chance to give him the best of everything, which any mother this day and time would want. Most mothers, hope for the best education for their child or wanting them to become president one day. Moses's name means "drawn out," which refers to taking him out of the water.

In 1 Chronicles 41:8, she married Mered the Judahite, Caleb's son, and joined the people of Israel. Miriam, Shammali, and Ishoah were born in this union.

Pharaoh's daughter's husband was against the spies, and she rebelled against her father's teachings. She laid down her life but didn't forsake her religion. She believed in God. She refused to accept or support anything to do with idolatry.

In Jewish tradition, she was exiled by the Pharaoh for bringing Moses the Levite into the house and claiming him as her own. Moses's great resurrection was his faith when he became older. He refused to be called the son of Pharaoh's daughter. He chose rather to suffer affliction with the people of God. He'd rather have Christ's greater riches/treasures in Egypt. He felt it wasn't robbery to be equal with God.

God reward her action. Knowing Moses wasn't her biological son. Letting her knows, she called Moses her son, just like He called her daughter, knowing she not biological to Him. Yet you called him your son, you are not my daughter. He also called her Judahite (or Jewish) wife because she was an Egyptian. During the time of the plagues, she wasn't affected because she was living the lifestyle of the Israelites, the children of the covenant and heirs of the promise which God made to Abraham.

The Faith (Bit-Yah) and her husband the adoptive parents of Moses between the two there was a mixture of unbelief. God overlooked their different, but through the grace of faith, He used Pharaoh's daughter to keep the rescuer of Israel, Moses alive. God always uses whoever and whatever is available in all sorts of incidents such as this. In this incident, He used Pharaoh's daughter to keep the rescuer of Israel, Moses, alive.

Here is a thought: being disrespectful honoring one's parents does not mean one is obligated to follow in their lifestyle of belief if it isn't corresponding with following Gods ways. Amen!

The Atonement

Year 2015

Praise the Lord. I gived honor to God who is the head of my life, and I give honor to all of you.

I want to speak a little on the Atonement of the Jewish holy day, Yom Kippur. *Yom Kippur* means "atonement" in the language of Hebrew. This holy day also included me and you because we are the sons and daughters of God. This is the day man, us, make things right, meaning this is a time of forgiveness. Jesus said that this day was made for man and not the Sabbath. You can read that in Mark 2:27–28. In the Old Testament, the Sabbath, or what we call the seventh day of the week, would be our Saturday. But most Christians observe Sunday as the day of worship because Christ's resurrection was on the first day of the week. This was also called a rest day.

Now doing Yom Kippur it is observe by Jews on the Sabbath, which is Saturday, but most Christian observes Sundays of worshipping at this appointed time. In the month of September doing the new moon Rosh Hashanah is New Year Day and a New Beginning for the Jews.

Christians start Yom Kippur at sun up or sun down, usually 6 a.m. to12 p.m. We start our fasting by giving up drinking and eating. Having nothing but water and praying all day. This is a time when we need to humble ourselves so we can hear from God. There shouldn't be any celebration, such as partying and weddings. This is God's time. This is the season. The time for sowing our seeds and the time to sacrifice for harvesting of our blessings of receiving favors and showing respect.

Jesus wants us to prosper and have peace. So we need to start planting. Jesus wants to do great things for us. If you go to Joel 2:21–32, you will see the seven blessings that are just for you.

These verses speak of the former rain, which is the first rain to start the developing of your seeds, and the latter rain is the spring rain, which allows your plant to be at its fullest. (1) This called the double blessing. There is this old saying that said, double for your troubles.

Now when doing Yom Kippur, God works fast. He takes time out. Usually, when we plant the seed, it takes time to grow, then we harvest, but when doing Yom Kippur, we plant the seeds, and in no time, we harvest. Amen!

(2) We have financial breakthroughs. Back in the Old Testaments, cows, livestock, corn, grapes to make wine, and the oil was money for people. In Joel 2, it's telling us that we will be over-flowed; we will be blessed abundantly.

You know, whatever the devil has stolen from you, you will get back. (3) It will be restored. It doesn't even have to be money, it could be your ideas, or thoughts in your mind. You could be thinking about going back to school or just travel. The devil tells you to wait and do it later when you're capable of doing it now. Also doing Yom Kippur can get you back your peace of mind.

(4) Now the Miracle of Wonderous: When we're wondering how something going to happen for us, and feeling it's going to take a miracle for it to take place, but it happens. the Lord supplies our needs, and He is an on-time God.

(5) Everywhere you go, God's divine presents is there with you. You another's may feel like certain things is not possible to happen at that present time, but it happens. Afterwards you may be saying things such as: It was God, But God, or OMG. He is there even in your rights or wrongs.

(6) There will be a blessing upon your family, not just you but your children, spouse, and anyone living with you. God wants them to be prosper too. I do say at times that I am blessed because my children have been blessed with something.

(7) Let's not forget the blessings of deliverance. We want everybody to be saved, and God will save them like he has saved me and you. Just keep praying for them with faith in the name of Jesus. Amen!

In the time of Yom Kippur, you will go through trials and tribulations. The devil will try you. Just think about it, have you even thought about all of the real bad weather we have during the month of September all around the world? We even had 9/11 going on. Don't let the devil throw you off. Just stay focused on Jesus.

You can start your fasting by preparing yourself with drinking more water and having less food than usual a few days ahead of time. Always take medicine as instructed. Even if you need to eat a little food with your medicine, it's okay. Save on the spending by not going to the shopping malls or eating out. Save for your sacrificial offering. You know tithing and offering are two different things (read Deuteronomy 16:16). It tells us to not come empty handed but come and give what we are able to give. God will give you instructions, just pray and ask.

However, as you go forth with your offering and prayers, go with asking and giving forgiveness and thankfulness in your heart. Keep praying with faith in Jesus's name. Amen!

Again, here's the list of the seven blessings for you:

1. Giving you double
2. Financial breakthrough
3. Restoration
4. Miracle of Wonderous
5. Divine presents
6. Blessing over family
7. Deliverance

Everyone will have thirty days to partake in Yom Kippur sacrificial offering. Don't miss out on your blessings. Stay blessed!

Thanksgiving Is More than Thanksgiving Day

Praise the Lord. I would like to thank the Lord for this day, especially on this special day, the day of giving thanks, because He is worthy of praise, honor, and to be glorified.

Thanksgiving is more than Thanksgiving Day. I want to speak on Thanksgiving Day.

First, I would like to ask, do we really recognize the season of Thanksgiving? The season is our daily living. Thanksgiving is more than Thanksgiving Day. Thanksgiving isn't about just eating and saying a short grace at the table or going for the leftover by making sandwiches for a few rounds afterward. It's not even about being with your family and friends and having joy and laughter for just that day. The joy should come every day. Amen!

Peace is a blessing. We need to stay in peace and to stay in peace, we should stay in praise, have gratitude, and continue to be grateful. During Thanksgiving, be thankful. Remembering God is a God of blessing. Serve the Lord, you and your family. Remember also that if God isn't in your home, you want have peace. God covers your children. He is about peace and protection.

Get on doing your Father's business. Believe, receive, and use your faith. Yes, it is God's will. You know, believing is doing it. He wants you to be victorious and have peace. Don't complain and mourn about your trials and tribulations. It takes work and work is the proof of your belief.

He blesses us with promotion and increases. God came to give us a bountiful life. Thank God for everything and walk in faith because that is what He really wants. Have you thought on gratitude?

Gratitude is a way of receiving your blessing. If you're not grateful in the small things or what you already have, why should God give you more for you not to be grateful? Be grateful for the small things as much as how grateful you are for the big things that has happened to you. Thank God each and every day as you go through your daily life.

I am asking you today to think on these things: clothes on your back, shoes on your feet, roof over your head, even the homeless should be thankful to have a box to sleep in. People going to jail could be saving them from other things, such as addiction or being killed. You might have a small paycheck, but it is better than having nothing at all. You might have lost a mother or a father, but you still got one or the other. Praise God. Be thankful and grateful for what you have.

Just remember this as you go through even in the middle of it all, you are intact and God gives us life and godliness. He knows your heart. Go to God. Confess that you are blessed. Thank God that the blood still works.

To have victory, just use all the tools God has given you. The devil will go to your thoughts, your mind. We have the mind of Christ. Go by the Word of Christ. Listen to the Holy Spirit. Live in the Holy Spirit. The Holy Spirit has a way to walk you through. Stay focused with the help of Jesus.

Christ warned we may be deceived to be unworthy of trust, but we may place all our trust and confidence in Him (Matt. 10). You know, believing is a decision, and faith is what you believe. Mark 11:24 reads: "Therefore I say to you what things so ever ye desire, when ye pray, believe that ye receive them and ye shall have them."

The more you learn about Jesus, the more you want to learn about Him. Your inner man will change. Jesus loves people. Walk in love. Walk in faith and love and have patience. We have all types of people in the world, even people in bad situations. We must use all these things.

Don't pray for God to be with you, He is already there. He will never leave you. Don't separate yourself from your loved ones. They're important to God. We should expand ourselves and be more grateful than yesterday. Let your light shine before men that they may see your good works and glorify the Lord. Thank Him of the goodness He has done for you and thank Him and be grateful. Amen!

FAITH, HEALING, AND MIRACLES

During my healing, going back and forth to doctors, I thanked the Lord each day for everything that He has done in my life, especially in healing me each time. Through these miracles of healing, I learned to have more faith and to pray, which I didn't think I knew how to at those times, trusting in the Lord more and more on any circumstance that came my way: sickness, food, finances, shelter, clothing, anything. I truly believe He will take care of me and my loved ones every day.

I used to think healing was just for the sick (health), but it is more than that. It's a deliverance from bondage of habits, misbeliefs on religion, or just understanding God. Faith is merely believing that God will do all things, which He said in His Word. He would do if we would only believe. "If thou canst believe, all things are possible to them that believe" (Mark 9:23).

Every Christians has equal rights, and it is God's will and desire that each of His children claim and accept all His blessings. Every person should pray and receive the answer. Jesus said everyone that asks receives (Matt. 7:8). Another important thing to keep in mind is that to be saved, you must do your own repenting, your own believing, your own confession, your own accepting, your own receiving, your own claiming, then you will be healed. We must talk faith. We shouldn't give in to satan's confession. Stop talking defeat. Stop talking sickness, weakness, disease, and trouble. They are from the devil. As long as we are praising satan's works, we cannot expect to maintain victory.

When we have faith, we no longer moan and groan, you praise and rejoice. Faith talks positively, faith sings joyfully. Faith prays confidently. We must remember the thief (satan) comes to steal, to kill, and destroy. "Jesus said: I am come that they might have life, and that they might have it more abundantly" (John 13:10). We must know that satan is the god of this world (2 Cor. 4:4).

There are different types of demon spirits, just like different type of people. They have personalities, they manifest own personalities in the person they prosses. Demons talk, they are intelligent, resist surrender, may call for reinforcements, cause diseases, but demons recognize and obey those who have power over them. People should know there is power in the name of Jesus. Christ emphasized His promise, "If you shall ask anything in my name, I will do it, by repeating it twice" (John 14:12–14). He did not exclude healing from this promise. Anything includes healing. This promise is for all. The one important thing to remember about healing the sick is that once you have accepted Christ as Savior, you are a child of God and have the right to fulfillment of any and all of God's promises. I thank the Lord for all trials and tribulations I go through because it brings me closer to Him. I thank Him for leaving me as a witness for Him to tell His story, His healing, and the miracles that I receive from Him. I say thank you, Lord.

To Receive God's Blessings

The scripture Luke 9:12–17 brought back to my memory an experience that I once had. I had an assignment to do for one of my classes. It was to experience missionary work. A group of us, about twelve, was asked to go feed the homeless at a shelter. First, we had to figure out what we were going to feed them and how to purchase the items we needed to do this assignment. We went to different store owners and others, letting them know we needed their help. Everyone gave bread and items to make spaghetti, forks, bowls, napkins, and paper bags. We had a fellowship church that was kind enough to let us use their kitchen that was big enough for us to prepare the food and pack everything up. We transported the food by cars at the appointed time and place to meet up for the mission. When we arrived, people who were outside the building were given food that was not expected. We guessed about how many people we might have to feed.

After entering the building, we prayed over the food being served to those that was in the line. As we were serving, it looked like we're running out of bread to serve, so we started breaking the bread into smaller pieces, and surely there was more than enough to serve. I felt my experience should be told to help build someone's faith. "With God nothing shall be impossible" (Luke 1:37). Not forgetting other scripture such as John 3.22:

Whatsoever we ask we receive.

James 4:2:

Ye have not, because ye ask not.

and Matthew 7:7:

Ask and it shall be given.

This mission taught me about faith and He do supply all our needs. Others were blessed with a meal. If my instructor wasn't trying to teach us different lessons in one lesson, we wouldn't have been asked to do the assignment, and no one would have received the blessings the Lord had given us, like the disciples and the five thousand men.

SARAI AND ABRAM

Sometimes things seem impossible to people, like it did to Sarai and Abram. People just want to wait for things to happen, just want to do them in their own time, just want wait on God's time.

Sarah hadn't borne a child for Abram. Thinking she couldn't, she told her husband Abram to go into her maidservant, whose name was Hagar (Gen. 16:3). During that time, Abram, at the age of eighty-six, did what his wife wanted him to do. Hagar, the maidservant, conceived a child. Abram's wife despised Hagar and wanted her out of their life. She asked Abram to ask Hagar to leave, which she did (Gen. 16:4–46). Later Hagar returned, still pregnant, but obeyed what the Lord told her to do. Having a covenant between the Lord and herself, the child shall be taken care of and shall be called Ishmael (Gen. 16:9).

Later in life, at the age of ninety, Sarai, who had become Sarah, and Abram, who had become Abraham, at the age of one hundred, was blessed with a child together named Isaac.

This shows that God does things in His time, and also keeps His covenant always (Gen. 17:19).

PART 2

Hope

Hope is a feeling that what is wanted will happen. Hope is a desire accompanied by expectation. It is to want and expect. A sure and steady faith in God's promises. The believer has hope in God's promise of salvation (1 Thess. 5:8), resurrection (Acts 26:6–7), and eternal life (1 Cor. 15:19–26).

Living Your Dreams

We can start by doing what Thessalonians 4:11 says,

> And that ye study to be quiet and to do your
> own business and work with your own hands.

Amen! Start by working with enthusiasm. Do all things in the name of the Lord. Psalm 37:5 says,

> Commit thy way unto the Lord; trust also
> in him; and he shall bring it to pass.

You should read the next one, also underneath verse 6, it says,

> And he shall bring forth thy righteousness
> as the light, and thy judgement as Noonday.

Remember looking for faults in someone or something, but the fault is of your own? We should check our own attitudes and serve others with gladness and the right spirit. Serve others well even if they're in your circle or outside of it. Care about the people around you. There are countless ways of achieving greatness of any road. Achieving one's maximum potential must be built on a bedrock of respect for the individual, commitment to excellence, and rejection of mediocrity. That means that even if someone is inferior or lower than you, you can never judge other people. We don't know what God has told them.

We need to be wise. Just saying we love Jesus doesn't make us wise. Have you really stopped and focused on what you really wanted and understood who you really are working for? We work for God, so commit your vision to the Lord.

Achieving education and going higher is something. It is possible to aim for many things because humans have a brain capable of doing three or four things at once. Expand your skills, exceed what is expected of you. God does above and beyond and does twice as much. Be a blessing to others. Set a goal by saying, "I will live my dream." Focus on what you really want. How about just dedicating or committing your work and life for God's purpose?

As we know it, James 1:8 said,

> A Doubled Minded Man is unstable in all his ways.

So how about you get a new birth, a new vision of your life and focus on it. You know people will go astray without a vision, and as it is also said,

> Where there is no vision, people perish. (Proverbs 29:18)

So remember in Habakkuk 2:2, it says,

> Write the vision and make it plain.

You also need to put the vision to work because without works, it's dead. Don't be just a hearer, be a doer. First, have a plan of action. Give thoughts on your plans and get God's blessing. Be prepared. Set a goal that you can measure. That's timing. Make a schedule, write it down. You know that is scripture make it plain (Amen!) read what you wrote daily. Put a picture to your vision and confess it. Get yourself healed. Walk in love, peace, be willing, and believe in Christ. "Trust the Lord with all thine heart and lean not unto thine own understanding, that is coming out of" (Prov. 3:5).

Do not forget to ask God what he wants you to do, how to do it, and when to do it. Humble yourself and listen, get a clear understanding, and be obedient. Don't be double-minded in your prayers, say what you actually want and believe and receive it. In your healing of illness, business, family issues, and in your wants, such as a car or a house because if you don't, it's really not praying.

The last thing I would like to speak on is this: God is love and faith is substances of things hoped for the evidence of things not seen. God knows you and your thoughts, and He's got a plan. In Isaiah 55:8, He said, "For my thoughts are not your thoughts neither are your ways my ways." Wouldn't it be nice to have a relationship with Jesus?

Entrepreneurship and Succeeding

Don't you know you already prosper when you have God in your life? God wants to give us favor. He really wants you to prosper and succeed, especially rising up to your destiny. He wants us to succeed from illness and from emotional hurts. He wants better education, jobs, business opportunity, increase of finances, better home situation, and also wants you to get closer to Him. How about dedicating your work to God? Proverbs 16:3 says, "Commit thy works unto the Lord, and thy thoughts shall be established."

You know people will go astray without a vision and as it is also said Proverbs 29:18, "Where there is no vision, people perish." Habakkuk 2:2 It says, "Write the vision and make it plain." Put a picture to your vision and confess it. Put it to work because without work, it's dead. Don't be just a hearer, be a doer. Give thought on your plans and get God's blessing.

In my opinion, we need more of God. Spend time in the Scripture. Spend more quality time, an intimate time, with God. We need to just focus on God more. Get rooted and grounded in the Lord. Start early in the morning. Get prayed up before your day gets started. Thank God for everything. Sometimes we have to adjust our schedule to have time with the Lord. You might need to go to bed a little earlier than others in the house to wake up even earlier than anyone else in the house to have that alone time with the Lord. You need to find a special meeting place in your home to have that alone time in your relationship with God each day. Whatever it takes, just do it.

Make a schedule for yourself, don't forget to include time for your family, and give yourself a time out. You can't have success without a successful mind. Don't forget God created everything. Plan a trip with family or a vacation just for yourself. If you want to go to a show or go dancing, go do so. Just remember that Colossians 3:2 says, "Set your affection on things above, not things on the earth." Also don't just quit your present job when in business for yourself, thinking you have enough to survive on when in the truth, you really don't.

Don't be selfish; share or give away, volunteer some of your time. Sometimes you do have to encourage yourself in your doings because others might not agree. Get involve in networking and media. When in business, you may need a coach, mentor, or pastor. Be around successful people doing things you do and involving your plans or vision.

Wouldn't it be nice to have a relationship with Jesus as a coach, mentor, or pastor, knowing in Hebrews 13:5 He said, "I will never leave thee, nor forsake you"?

Having Favor

Some people nickname Fridays as Favor Friday. Don't you know God is a God of blessing? His mercy is new every day. Don't you know "having favor" is the meaning of friendly, regarding approval, a kind act? It's a small gift or a token. It's to approve or like, to partiality, to support to make easier. It's to help, to do kindness for, to assemble, to use gently, and the advantage of. We are truly blessed for having the favor of God upon us this day and forevermore. There is no lack or limits with God. Amen! We are heirs of God, and we are entitled to everything. God is a good God.

In 2 Thessalonians 5:24, it says, "Faithful is he that calleth you unto also will do it." God sets open doors. All God needs is your faith. He is your helper. He will never leave you, nor forsake you. Remember Jesus Christ is the same yesterday, today, and forever. Amen!

It is the things that make you uncomfortable that limit things in your life. God sends opportunity. God wants to do things for you, but sometimes it will take you out of your comfort zone. Coming out of your comfort zone you, do have to pay a price.

God isn't going to tell you or show you anything new until you do what He already told you to do. Do what you know to do. Take care of it. Sometimes, it is because of what you didn't do that will limit you. God uses the foolish things to find the wise. When God does things, He does it well. He is a rewarder.

God waits on you to get involve. It's not until you do the hard things that it becomes easy. You have to invest. Faith without work is dead. We do want things, but we don't know how to receive it or get it. We must stop being pitiful. We don't grow up until things are taken from us. Sometimes your answer comes when you're down.

God created you and you will come out. You have to walk through it. God is about filling His will, not ours. There is a blessing in it. We need to believe in God's favor. Thank our Father God for prosperity. Stop putting limits on yourself. Remember there is no limits on God. Psalms 35:27 says, "Let them shout for joy, and be glad, that favor my righteous cause: yea, let them say continually, Let the Lord, be magnified, which hath pleasure in the prosperity of his servant." Amen!

How Many Steps Will You Take?

I give honor to God, give Him all my praise, and glorify His holy name.

My subject is how many steps will you take? Too responding and believing. We all know both words are approving and action words that must be put to work in each of our lives. Such as Jesus said in John 9:4–4, "I must work the works of him that sent me, while it is day: the night cometh, when no man can work. As long as I am in the world, I am the light of the world."

Have we really thought about what we are saying or doing? Are we saying and doing the right things? Are we really agreeing with God? We need to take what God has given us or said about us and putting it in use, not just sitting on it. Just like in the story of the blind man when Jesus made spate and anointed the eyes of the blind man with the clay and sent the man to the pool of Siloam for healing, which was an underground tunnel with water from a spring. This was a long distance outside of the city. This man is the one who responded and believed. He traveled while still blind to receive his healing. This was work in action. He also told about the goodness of the Lord after his healing. After his transformation, he said, "Now I can see." Amen!

We also don't want to forget the story about the ten lepers. The lepers asked Jesus from a distance for mercy when he entered their village. Jesus told them to go show themselves to the priests. Jesus sent, them to show that they had been spiritual cleanse that shows it is true. But as they were walking or taking steps with this disease, they were being healed. Only one realized what really happened. He returned to give thanks and glory to God. Jesus told the Samaritan that his belief made him whole. He was the only one who responded with belief, putting both in action when he glorified the Lord.

I also want to speak a little on the subject the Father, the Son, and the Holy Ghost. To me, this is a shorter way to healing than the twelve step programs, not saying each has their own purpose in this world. I myself have seen the works of such programs through others, but it takes a little longer. I have learned that even the twelve steps uses the Holy Bible, the Word. Amen!

As people are recovering using the twelve steps, they're finding the truth and principles through the Scripture and discovering what God has to say about overcoming or gaining new direction in their life. I am saying one quote that comes to mind: "You can't keep it unless you give it away." Having to receive healing and spiritual renewal, we retain them only as we offer to help others. The last works of the twelve steps mean that if people are spiritually transformed, they will begin to observe the difference in their financial living, relationships, communication, even in their sexual conduct, just to name a few. The transformation would be real or evidently true. Just like the Samaritan, it was real, and he was the evidence that his transformation was true.

The book of Proverbs gives instruction for our daily living. One is saying, "Attend to my words, incline thine ears unto my sayings." Jesus answers in one point of the Bible, "My Father, worketh hitherto, and I work." Amen!

If only we can work on humbling ourselves and start believing and trusting in the Lord. The Holy Spirit will always give you the right answers, but you must respond right. Just like the blind man and the leper, they both heard the Word, they both worked with responding and believing. It was just that easy.

Just ask and it shall be given you, seek and ye shall find; knock; and it shall be opened unto you. (Matt. 7:7)

Let your light so shine before men, that they may see your good works, and glorify your father which is heaven. Amen! (Matt. 5:16)

So how many steps will you take? How about the shorter steps, the Father, the Son, and the Holy Ghost? Amen!

Now for those who heard this message and who likes to be renewed and healed and transform, also to those who believe and trust our Lord Savior, it's easy, please humbles yourselves and repeat after me:

Heavenly Father, I come to you acknowledging you as God. I confess as a sinner and believe that your son, Jesus, was sent here on earth, died, and was raised in three days, sacrificed himself for my sin so I can receive eternal life. I ask you, Jesus, will you be my Lord and Savior and lead my steps in all areas of my life? I receive you as my Lord Savior. I pray all things in Jesus's name. Amen!

Rise Up to Your Destiny

Praise the Lord. The subject that is on my mind is to rise up to your destiny. The unavoidable fate that has the power to determine the outcome. The question here is are you ready to rise up?

Knowing no one can rise up for you, myself included, we must pick up, clean up, and clear out our minds. Just take full responsibility of our own destiny. I am referring out of the book of Colossians 3:6–15 (King James Version):

> (6) For which things' sake the wrath God cometh on the children of disobedience:
>
> (7) In the which ye also walked some time, when ye lived in them.
>
> (8) But now ye also put off all these; anger, wrath. Malice, blasphemy, filthy, communication out of your mouth.
>
> (9) Lie no one to another, seeing that ye have put off the old man with his deeds;
>
> (10) And have put on the new man, which is renewed in knowledge after the image of him that created him:
>
> (11) Where there is neither Greek nor Jew, circumcision nor uncircumcision, Barbarian, Scythian, bond nor free: but Christ is all and all.
>
> (12) Put on therefore, as the elect of God, holy and beloved, bowels of mercies, kindness, humbleness of mind, meekness, longsuffering;

(13) Forbearing one another, and forgiving one another, if any man has a quarrel against any, even as Christ forgave you, so also do ye.

(14) And above all these things put on charity, which is the perfectness.

(15) And let the peace of God rule in your hearts, to the which also ye are called in one body; and be thankful.

Let this reading be a blessing to all who has heard. Amen!

Are we really ready to rise up? I'm letting you know that by doing these things, we must do some work. Titus 3 speaks that we, ourselves, are sometimes foolish, disobedient, and we deceive. To name a couple more, we envy and hate one another, but to rise up, we must pick up, clean up, and clear out our mind. Now how can we when have so much going on in our lives? Well, we must change. We can start by being godly, being greater, and being grateful. We should learn to maintain good works for necessary uses, avoid foolish questions about racism, whether who's right or wrong or just struggling. It's not worth it. These are the few things we can clear out of our minds.

Now there are two things comes to my mind in order to rise up to our destiny. We must learn forgiveness and communication. Ephesians 4:32 also says,

And be ye kind one to another, tender-hearted, forgiving one even as God for Christ sake hath forgiven you.

Let's us also not even forget,

Let no corrupt communication proceed out of your mouth. (Ephesian 4:29)

We should expand ourselves, be greater than yesterday. Be grateful by showing action and think before speaking. That is how to be godly. Wake up or rise up with Jesus on your mind.

Just pray and talk to God. Get a relationship with Him. Be thankful of the goodness He's done for you.

There is a scripture telling us about when we enter into our closet and shut the door. How can we shut the door when things kept falling out? We haven't Picked up, cleaned up, or cleared out some things. Listen to this:

> But thou, when thou prayest, enter into thy closet, and when thou hast shut the door, pray to the Father which is in secret, and thy Father which seeth in secret shall reward thee openly. But when ye pray use not vain repetitions, as the heathen do. (Matt 6:6)

Amen!

Praying, no good things on someone, eye for an eye or tooth for and tooth.

God wants to give favors. He wants you to prosper, to succeed, especially when rising up to your destiny. He wants you to succeed in your healing from illness, from emotional hurt. He wants for you to have better education, job, business opportunity, increase of finances, and better home situation. Also, you are getting closer to Him. You're already Prospering when you have God in your life. Just have the attitude of wanting to pick up, clean up, and clear out things. Don't make it a chore, make it a choice. Amen!

We can start cleaning up by doing what 1 Thessalonians 4: 11 says, "And that ye study to be quiet, and to your own business and work with your own hands." Remember, looking for faults in someone or something is a fault of your own. Learn to forgive yourself. Forgiveness is power, you have the authority to use it. "And when ye stand praying forgive, if ye have ought against any; that your Father also which is in heaven may forgive your trespasses." (Mark 11:25)

I leave these questions to you. In your plans, what will be your outcome in rising up to your destiny? Will you have a better communication with others and with God? Will you have forgiveness in your heart even for yourself? Be more godly by loving others as God loves you. Be greater by making room for better things. Be grateful, knowing God is please when "the Word," goes out it shall not turn void, but shall accomplish and it will prosper things where it's sent too."

Are you thankful? I know I am thankful for all things unto God the Father, in Jesus's name.

I hope, like me, you are going to pick up, clean up, and clear out a pathway to your destiny by welcoming a relationship of love with the Lord our Savior. Amen!

Don't you worry about making mistakes, God looks at and knows your heart. He loves you. Don't argue with Him! God loves you through Jesus Christ. He has made a clear way back to God. There is no other path or way.

Now, please for those who wants this wonderful outcome, repeat after me:

I believe, Heavenly Father, you raised Jesus Christ form the dead, and He is alive and well-seated at your right hand in heaven. I repent from my sins and choose to follow and obey Jesus Christ as my Lord and Savior. I ask you, Jesus Christ, to be the Lord of my life and lead me in all areas of my life. Jesus Christ, I receive you as my Lord and Savior with all my heart and believe that you are my King and my God. In Jesus's name, amen!

For those who repeated this, you're saved and on the right path to a wonderful outcome. God bless you all!

CHRISTMAS

The Three Wise Men

P raise the Lord.

This is from the book of Matthew 2:1–12, a short story of the Three Wise Men.

The Three Wise Men, also known as the Three Kings, followed a bright star that led them to Bethlehem, where the Messiah was born. They accepted Jesus has their Savior.

We don't need to seek God; He isn't hiding from us. Instead, He wants to have an intimate relationship with each of us.

The Three Wise Men gave Jesus the kind of respect only God deserves: bowing before Him, worshipping Him, and presenting Him with gifts. He is the Son of the Living God and a great teacher. After the Three Wise Men met Jesus, they didn't go back the way they came. When we get to know Jesus Christ, we are changed forever and can't go back to our old ways. Amen!

I feel we all as Christian should let our light shine bright so we can help others find their way to our Lord Savior, just as the Three Wise Men found theirs. We know He isn't hiding; it's just that others need such a bright light like the shining star so they can see their way. Why not let your light shine so they can have such a relationship with God just like you? Let them receive their gifts from Him like you have. He is such an awesome teacher. Why not share what you have learned by our teacher Jesus Christ? They will never be the same. Tell your testimony on how good God has been to you. What a Christmas gift you can give someone by letting your light shine bright.

The Power of Vision

First of all, what is a vision? We must not forget that God's visions work through us. What is our real vision? Not thinking of a mission is a vision. Vision isn't a selfish desire but a selfish quest. A vision is used by a faithful servant of God. A vision is a special gift given to reflect a realist perspective. It's a dream that seems impossible to build on reality.

With a vision it helps the future that we receive clearly doing our current state of situations. Not mean that we should be lazy, No it something we pray for waited on and worked toward doing something about it. Most of all it is a team working together as a spiritual thing (conception).

Vision is so powerful that some people confuse mission with vision, forgetting that they need a vision first in order to have a mission in place. A mission is an action word. A mission is something you just keep working on. It seems that you're not getting anywhere because you just don't have a beginning or an ending for your mission. Also, you might be trying to accomplish your idea alone when it takes a team to make it work.

A vision is a gift from God that is given to you. God gives different skills each day. God's vision seems like a long-term vision in nature. Vision may outlive the visionary, which could be you. Fear not, His goals are eternal, not temporal. His knowledge and resources are unlimited, enabling us to pursue a vision for which He will be responsible in ending. God is always on time in vision and mission.

The Importance of Art in Church

First of all, I feel we need to remember the scripture: "Thou art worthy, O Lord. To receive glory and honor and power for thou hast created all things and for thy own pleasure they are and were created" (Rev. 4:11). The art is not for our own pleasure or for us to be so judgmental on how it is presented. Churches have taken arts out because it seems it could be deception to other people around them. God is unlimited. He made everything Himself, including foolish things. Snatching arts out putting it away like a capture animal we need to (Shaw-booah) all arts back in churches such as dance. Job 21:11, "They send forth their little ones like a flock and their children dance." This alone says a lot about God's love. Even children praise and worship Him in dancing.

Art performances shouldn't be judged so harshly, especially when we really don't understand the way it is presented to us. We also have to remember that satan is not a creator. He uses elements that are already here. Some art seem strange to people, especially those that are done out of the ordinary. "They take the timbral and harp and rejoice at the sound of the organ" (Job 21:12). That may seem strange. People are set into things in the old traditional way, the plain old Grandma's way. Having a fear of trying a new thing or not believing it could work out is not having enough faith in the Holy Spirit guiding us. Not believing can keep us from receiving blessings. "And things, whatsoever ye shall ask in prayer, believing, ye shall receive" (Matt. 21:22).

The Lord wants to reach everyone with His message. He sends different messengers and uses different methods of giving His message. For instance, there are five divine dances that are used for different situations. We have the intercessory (when the Holy Spirit communicates with the dancer and God is in control, the dancer expresses the will of God in the dance) and lyrical (a spiritual dance warfare dance it interprets in natural) as an example.

Those were just a couple of examples on how powerful art can be to us. All we have to do is invite God into our situations by clapping our hands (teqa) and be very loud and aggressive (shebach). We must present ourselves in a barak way no matter who we see. His message stays the same. No matter what art performance it's coming from, it never changes. We need to celebrate (halla), praise, and thank God more. We can't put the Holy Spirit in a box.

Art isn't just pretty, it's powerful. Art is a form of praise and worship. It is something we can hear and see. "Take a psalm and bring hither the timbral the pleasant harp with the psaltery" (Ps. 81:2–3). We know Jesus is the greatest communicator (Jer. 32:17–21). Jesus talked in word pictures.

It is very important for us to have art in churches. We can extol and magnify praises and worshipping in churches today. "We will rejoice in salvation, an in the set up our banners the Lord fulfill all thy petitions" (Ps. 20:5). If feeling we're Anointing of the ministry. Feeling the uplifting of our burdens being removed, knowing yokes are being destroyed and receiving the power of God, and knowing Elohim, our almighty powerful Creator, is pleased that we have retreated the gift of art in the churches. Knowing all things are created by Him and for Him. (Col. 1:16–17). I really feel art is very important in the churches.

Do You Want to Be Healed?

If you don't make a change, there won't be a change. You can't gain victory until you suffer: emotions, cruel people, rejection, depression, suicide, marriage problems. Answers come when you're in the pit. You don't grow up until things are taken from you. There is a blessing in the plan. God created you. You will come out. You have to work it out.

God is about filling His will, not ours. You shall live and not die. Ask God for a strategy. The devil will speak to you. Power is given to you by the higher power, "God". What you think is your rock bottom might not be your bottom. Keep living by faith, faith without work is dead. Your belief is in your action. God wants to give you the anointing in the old body. The change has to take place in you. It's a personal change. God wants to make a new you. What is it that you want?

If you want things to get better, God can make things better. He wants to take you to another level, but you have to be willing. You have to cooperate and be willing. God needs you to work with Him so you can move higher. He won't do it if you don't work with Him. He wants to work through you. Ask Him what He wants you to do. He will give you the power. He rearranges things. God is able to do things. Do what you know to do. He we will work with us. He can help us. You have to believe and act on your belief. You have to put your faith into your vision. You have to do your part.

Stop putting your life on hold. Sometimes you have to say no! You have to do the hard things for your life to become easier. Remember nothing is too hard for God. Depend on God; let Him help you. He will give you the strength. Go to Him for the plan so you can change. Glory to God.

Some things don't seem spiritual when you do them. Sometimes you may feel you're marching around a wall without God in your life. Walk in love, faith, and forgiveness. You don't have to make a God; He is a spirit. Seek, look, and behold means to watch and seek. You don't have to tell God how to do things. You don't change God. He is the same yesterday, today, and forever. God is faithful and a rewarder. Amen!

Focus, Pay Attention

Believe and focus on the Word. We have to get the intimate time with God. If we want to get healed, we have to pay attention to the Word of God. Begin to focus on His Word and don't just say you are going to do so. Don't start doubting. Take time to prepare yourself. The Word of God is true (John 17:17).

Live with God's Word. We have to get on track, focus. Change your mindset. Thank God for everything. Believe God if He says He is the healer, protector, the beginning, and the end. Whenever you can't talk out loud, pray in your mind. God gives us revelation on how to believe if we continue to focus on Him. Turn your situation over to God. He is true. Believe in your prayers.

God Is with You

He speaks from His spirit to your spirit. Be true in your spirit so you can hear. God is the way and the truth. Keep it real, not in your truth but in His truth. The spirit of the Lord is refreshing. He will refresh your soul. When people don't stop to get refreshed, they get burned out. We need to stop and have a Godly experience.

He is a Healer. He is the Way. He is the Truth. He is the Light.

There Is No Quitting in God

For where two or three are gathered together in thy name there am I in the midst of them. (Matt. 18:20)

Again I say unto you, that if two of you shall agree on earth as touching anything that they shall ask, it shall be done for them of my father which is heaven. (Matt. 19)

That ye may with one mind and one mouth glorify God, even the Father of our Lord Jesus Christ. (Rom. 15:6)

Now I beseech you, brethren, by the name of our Lord Jesus Christ that ye all speak the same thing, and that there be no division among you, but that ye be perfectly joined together in the same mind and in the same judgement. (1 Cor. 1:10)

God is a spirit; and they that worship him must worship him in the spirit and in true. (John 4:24)

Church

What is a Church?

You're the church
Represent the church
Speak in tongue
Speak a new tongue a new way
Walk in Love
Don't gossip
Tongue of faith
Powerful meeting is for believers
Hope comes by seeing
Faith comes by hearing
Preaching is making public and made known
Fancy clothes, crossing legs, isn't church
Testimony to you, for you, through you.

WHO DO WE WITNESS TO?

First we needed to go to God,

Asking for a fresh touch by giving you strength and to show you how.

Who do you witness to? Young generation step up, Love on them.

Train the younger generation.

We have responsibility to teach.

A witness is one who gives testimony regarding an event or another person's character.

Testimony, a declaration of truth, based on personal experience (Acts 4:20).

An older woman teaches a younger woman how to dress, talk, and what to do (Ruth 3:4–15).

Believers are empowered to serve as witness for Christ (Acts 1:8).

"Happy is the man that findeth wisdom, and the man that getteth understanding" (Prov. 3:12).

God Has a Plan

God has a plan for you. God is able. Don't compare your past to your present. Don't look behind you. When you're looking back, God's not able to do anything for you. He is not the God of "I was" or "I was not." The story of Lot, Abraham's nephew, is a great example. His uncle gave him the first choice on where to settle in Canaan's land. He chose the Jordan Valley that was fertile. Lot escaped the destruction of the city nearby. His wife looked back on Sodom, their possessions, and was turned into a pillar of salt. Jesus used her experience to warn of the dangers of delay and disobedience.

Lot was an ancestor of the Moabites and the Ammonites tribes, which became bitter.

PART 3

Love

Love is a strong affection for someone or something, a passionate affection of a person to another. It is an unselfish, benevolent concern for other people. (Cor. 13:4–7) To love God, with all thy heart, soul, and mind. Love your neighbors as well as yourself. (Matt. 22:37–40) These are two most important commands of Jesus. (John 13: 1; 15–13) Christ's sacrificial death was the supreme expression of love

Master of Our Focus

Praise the Lord. I give honor to all.

This is from the book of Proverbs 4:20–27, King James Version, and it reads:

> (20) My son attends to my words; incline thine ear unto my sayings.
>
> (21) Let them not depart from thine eyes; keep them in the midst of thine heart.
>
> (22) For they are life unto those that find them, and health to all their flesh.
>
> (23) Keep thy heart with all diligence, for out of it are the issues of life.
>
> (24) Put away from thee a forward mouth, and perverse lips put far from thee.
>
> (25) Let thine eyes look right on and let thine eyelids look strength before thee.
>
> (26) Ponder the path of thy feet and let all thy ways be established.
>
> (27) Turn not to the right Hand not to the left, remove thy foot from evil.

Let this reading be a blessing to those who have heard. Amen!

I would also like to speak a little on new birth that is regenerated by the Holy Spirit and produces a changed person (read John 3:5–8). All comes by the grace of God through faith in Christ rather than through your own efforts or good works. Being regenerated helps believers overcome the world and lead a victorious life (1 John 5:4–5) is a great example being regenerated.

Have you ever thought about the word *focus* or just using your focus? Do you realize focus is spiritual, and you need to stay focused on God to be successful? God has a plan, and His ways are higher than our ways, and His thoughts aren't our thoughts. Do not forgetting He is a spirit. Amen!

We need to tap into and focus on God more. Get rooted and grounded in the Lord. In order to straighten up, you need more words of God. Spend time in the Scripture. Spend more quality time, an intimate time with God. Start early in the morning. Get prayed up before your day and start thanking God for everything. God came to give you a bountiful life. He wants you to be victorious and have peace. Don't complain and mourn about your trials and tribulations. Focus, stay consistent, get your own self healed, and get your own life straightened out. Walk in love and peace. Be willing and believe. Be in Christ. Confess over what you want to talk to God. Ask Him what should you do, how to do it, and when you should do it.

We do need more Word of God than the word of the world, like news. We need to take heed of what we hear. We shouldn't be overtaken by evil. Don't focus on evil, such as shootings and murders. Focus on the good and don't talk about negative things.

Overcome wickedness. Take dominion over it and use your power of authority. The news will have an effect on you. You will need a comeback, so don't insert it.

Stay focused. Did you know looking is focus? Remember the old saying out of sight out of mind? Right now, I want to bring you back to Proverbs 4:25: "Let thine eyes look right on and let thine eyelids look straight before thee." Why not take a stare at the words and incline your ear unto the Lord's sayings? We need to be wise, and just Loving Jesus doesn't make us wise. Have you really stopped and focused on what you really want? How about taking a new look on where you are going in your life? As it is said in James 1:8, "A Double Minded Man is unstable in all his ways." So how about getting a new birth, a new vision of your life, and focus on it? You know people will go astray without a vision, and as it is also said, where there is no vision, people perish. So we need to put the vision to work. Without work, it's dead. Don't be just a hearer, be a doer.

Now some of us do get "overspiritual," and part of the reason is we haven't been taught on how to apply the Scripture into our lives, especially in our churches. We need to know God is a particular God. In John 14:6, Jesus gives us a foundation. He said, "I am the way, the truth, and the life. No man cometh unto the Father, but by me."

The smallest thing that we sometimes ignore is usually the foundation. You have to act and do your part because others can't do it for you. The Bible said to write your vision, meaning your plans, your hopes, and dreams. Get on doing your Father's business, write it down, believe in it, receive it, and use your faith. Yes, it is God's will. Believing is doing it. The work is the proof of your belief. It's easy to blame things on God and others when things don't happen. It's an excuse to bail out.

God wants you to increase and have prosperity, and don't you know we are free of curses? Have you noticed that churches talk about money more than they talk about heaven? Churches are so divided. Most people don't understand other people who just pray for increase. Jesus is rich. We get mixed messages about finances in our Christian life.

If you read Matthew 25, it's speaks of lack and prosperity. It tells about the five women who had enough and the other five who didn't. Some people misunderstand the word *talent* in this scripture. The word *talent* means "money." In Matthews, it shows you that God expects increase from your finances. Money has a mission, and the mission is to help people. Remember nothing is lacking if you live in the will of God. We must be masters of our focus.

It could be God's idea. We need to stand on the promises of God and don't run to and fro or in and out, be focused. People quit when things starts to develop. You should make a way for things to manifest. Choose your thoughts; God tells the truth.

You can cast out the devil's images. He will give you the thought of you being too old. He will tell you your children are nothing, and he will continue to put fear into you. But he is a liar.

Now I am guilty of this here. Sometimes we want to speak to our leader, our pastor, trying to get a right answer or a right-now prayer, but we do not go to them because we don't want them to know what's really going on in our life. Just remember this, as you go through, even in the middle of it all, you still are intact, and God gives us life and godliness. He knows our hearts.

Go to God, confess. Thank God that His blood still works. The seed of the righteous shall be delivered. Confess your vision. Master your focus about your finances, marriage, children, your health issues, even your ministry. So confess it, decree it, stand on the Word, and put your thoughts and your mind on Jesus. He is the foundation. Amen! So whatever God tells you to do or choose for you to do, take control and finish it. You know promotion don't come until you pass the test. So thank God again in all trials and tribulations. Keep an upgraded attitude. You can upgrade from where you are.

You can't be blessed by keeping on asking people to pray for you to be blessed. Why not be a blessing to someone else? Strengthen up if you mess up.

In Psalms 1, there are four words that stand out to me:

1) *Walketh*—You can say kind words to others as you walk by them.
2) *Standeth*—You can give attention to others even while you are standing in the Word.
3) *Sitteth*—You are really not paying attention. Get up and pick up your bed; don't just sit there.
4) *Scornful*—Talking about people, complaining, or gossiping.

Don't be in the negative. These are areas that you can strengthen up if you mess up. Don't be double-minded in your prayer. Say exactly what you want and believe and receive it. Believe and receive in your healing of illness, a car, family issues and job. Because if you don't believe in it, that isn't really praying.

Don't forget to ask God what He wants you to do, how to do it, and when to do it. Listen. Get a clear understanding and be obedient. When God shows you a picture or gives you a vision, put your mind on the image. A picture is worth a thousand words. Remember you have a part to do, and if you don't agree with it, it won't happen. God wants you to see what is coming, and you can see it with the clear vision.

My way of thinking is like baking a cake. You have a picture or an imagine on how it should look. You have the ingredients written down, following it. But if you miss one or two ingredients by not following the direction or setting the timer wrong, it's not going to come out right. It might not even rise up high. All because you had a better way of doing it, you messed the cake up. Now you need to start fresh to get it right by following the directions.

Speaking biblical, think about Joshua and Noah. They both were given direction on what, how, and when to do something. Think about Noah and the Ark he built. If he had not followed the direction that was given, they all could have drowned.

You have a chance if you mess up. Go to God. Go do things in order. It's His thoughts and His way. Be patient because He is an on-time God. So when we mess up, it doesn't mean we can't strengthen up. We know the Holy Spirit produces a change person by the grace of God through faith, and being regenerated helps believers overcome the world and lead a victorious life. So stay focused with the help of Jesus. Amen!

Let us all close our eye and look straight up to Thee. And for those who had ears to hear and wants to be regenerated with a fresh start and straighten up what you messed up and felt like you couldn't, raise your hands and, by the grace of God, with faith, all you have to do is ask and confess. Repeat after me:

> Heavenly Father, I come to you acknowledging you as God. I confess as a sinner and believe that your Son, Jesus, was sent here on earth, died, and had risen in three days. He sacrificed Himself for my sin so I can receive eternal life. I ask you, Jesus, will you be my Lord and Savior and lead my steps in all area of my life? I receive you as my Lord Savior. I pray all things in Jesus's name, amen!

Now for those who said this prayer, you're regenerated by the grace of God and born anew. Amen!

GIVING YOUR FAITH A VOICE

I would like to speak to you on giving your faith a voice. Now we must know we first have to fill our mouth with faith.

Now, as a Christian, we need to be careful of our mouth. As you know, God is a speaking spirit. We are made in His image. God is a living God and He is alive. We know the dead don't talk. Amen.

In James 2:20, it is asking if you want to know a foolish man. (women too) Amen!

That faith without work is dead. Now in James 3:10, it tells us, "Out of the mouth proceedeth blessing and cursing." Today I am trying to encourage you to give your faith a voice. In order to do so, remember the Bible is a love letter to the Jews, which includes me and you, the Gentiles. Amen! Also, I want to remind you that God is love and the Word, and the Word is truth. Amen!

In the love letter, Jesus said, "Have faith in God," and He also said, "Thou canst believe all, all things are possible to him that belie-veth." Words are life speaking. We live by the Word, so we need to check on our life. We need to agree with God. He created life. He said we can have a bountiful life. So just start everyday by thanking God for all things and repent, if necessary. After checking ourselves, we realize that we are all not perfect. Amen! God gives us the author-ity to call on things into exist.

Blessed are those who believe and confess. For those who believe, they are healed. Stand on your healing. Even when the pain comes back, confess your illness, saying I'm heal. Let the works in your heart come out of your mouth with belief.

We will be proof of God's will. Go with what God said. Trust in the Lord with all your heart and confess. Don't forget that in the love letter, it says that with His stripes, we are healed.

Give your faith a voice. Don't conform to things of the world. God will help you. He will make a way. You will prosper, but you must believe with *faith*. Don't line your mouth up with the devil. Hear no evil, speak no evil. Do not use curse with a curse.

Lean to God, not to your understanding. God knows things before it happens. Your own emotion is your own understanding. Emotion can get in the way of peace. In Isaiah 57:19, it reads this, "I create the fruit of the lips, peace, peace to him that is far off; and to him that is near saith the Lord, and I will heal him."

You know thanksgiving leads to peace, and peace leads to progress. Be grateful. Some people look back on things, such as someone who hurt them, a job lost, a home lost, a loss of a loves one, or a bad relationship. Don't look back, just praise Him. Remember, He knows before it happens, and He is a God of changes.

Do something meaningful in your life. Don't let ugliness come out of your mouth about others. Speak well and of people. Show them how you were blessed. Give testimonies on how God had been good to you. How he has watched over you through the nights. How He has put food on your table, clothes on your back, shoes on your feet, and a roof over your head. Speak about His mercy and grace, how He is teaching you to have forgiveness, and how you should use your mouth. Ephesians 4:29–30, 32 tells us,

> (29) Let no corrupt communication proceed out of your mouth, but that which is good to the edifying, that it may minister Grace unto the hearers.
>
> (30) Let all bitterness, and wrath, and anger, clamour, and evil speaking, be put away from you with malice.
>
> (32) And be ye kind one to another, tender hearted, forgiving one another, even as God for Christ sake hath for given you.

Amen!

Water your seeds with praises. Give your faith a voice. Edify with grace and forgive.

God has already given us authority to cast out and resist the devil. Put your mouth to work because the devil's job is to kill, steal, and destroy.

Cast all your cares on God. Don't be stressed. Walk in love, have patience. Ask God what to do or what to pray for when in need. Humble yourself so you can hear Him. Use the Scripture to apply your wants. Don't let your heart be troubled. Pray and thank God even when things are looking bad. "The more you pray" the more you trust and believe in Him.

You have to know God is not trying to pay you back on anything. We don't get on His nerves, and we don't have to beg like the women in the book of Matthew 15.

Men are afraid of God. Don't you know God is on your side? The cross is the proof that He is on your side.

Sometimes we feel we're all alone, but remember you're not alone, you have the favor of God. He will help you and strengthen you with abilities. Just keep loving God and people because without love, we are nothing.

Speak words of life assisted with faith, such as healing for yourself and others. Speak prosperity and blessings for a bountiful life. Give your faith a voice. Amen!

CHANGE

This is a message about change.

First, we have to go to God to be changed. God tells us what to think on. He tells us to think right things and have the right thoughts. You can read later about how the Holy Spirit produces a change in person (read John 3:5–8). Being regenerated helps believers overcome the world and lead a victorious life. All comes by the grace of God through faith in Christ.

Some people say God is a mean God. Some people are scared of God. God is a sweet God and lovable God. People do have the wrong thoughts about God. Remember, He loves you the same as He loves Jesus. Jesus Himself ask God to do, so God is just like Jesus. The Holy Spirit is the power of God. He did get angry before but sworn He won't again. (Read Isaiah 54:7–10 and verse 13.)

When Jesus spoke to God the Father, He spoke to Him on a different level, calling God Abba Father, which means "Daddy." God is our daddy because He adopted us as His children. Read this in Roman 8:15–16, and as you read it, notice the capital *S* on the word *Spirit*, it means that the Holy Spirit has a whole different meaning than the word *spirit* with the small letter *s*.

If you're scared of God, then that really isn't a real relationship because a relationship is love. God is love and His Word is true. Tell other people about the good news, that Jesus paid the price for us and our sins and nothing shall separate us.

We can change negative thoughts. If not, we will have negative results. Have thoughts of power, victory, and even forgiveness. What's in your mind is in your heart. That is your inner man. In Proverbs 23:7, you will read how your heart thoughts could be draw from heart. Don't let negative thinking push you around. "Greater is He that is in you" (1John 4:4). Free your mind and the rest will follow. You must change to have the right thoughts. To have God's will of love there's nothing shall separate us from His Love. (Roman 8:35–39). Don't you know the love of God will grow bigger? So keep believing and hoping, especially when you are hoping for something. The devil will try to take your hope away. Keep casting those thoughts down (read 2 Cor. 10:5), such as "I can't." Keep your hope alive. Remember, "Hope maketh not ashamed" (Rom. 5:5). Please remember Bible hope is having a promise from God. God wants us to have abundant life. Such as Prosperity, homes or be in good health, we always hope and pray for all. Bible hope is different from the world's hope, such as playing the lottery or when you go to the casino, hoping you will win. Keep the Bible hope alive. God watches over His promises. With God, all hope is possible. You can do all things through Christ (Rom. 12:12). Rejoice in hope.

Every day is a good day. This is the day the Lord has made. Psalms 23 says, "Surely goodness and mercy shall follow me all the days of my life." Don't feel like something bad always happens to you. Start thinking something good always happens to you and your family.

Resist the devil. Don't feed the devil with negative thoughts. Don't give the devil a place. The devil is a liar. Believe in the truth (Eph. 4:27). Stand on the Scripture. "For God hath not given us the spirit of fear, but of power, and of love and of a sound mind" (2 Tim. 1:7). A sound mind is being single-minded. You have the power to change. When we have a poor mind, that doesn't give God the glory. If you have a well and healthy mind, you will have a well and healthy body.

Don't have a fearful thought. Cast down those fearful imaginations. You feel bad because you think of it. Negative thinking will give you fear. Control your thoughts. You control the light and the darkness. Exercise your faith.

There shall no evil befall thee. (Ps. 91:10)

Let God be true. (Rom. 3:4)

So what you think about you will bring about. (Prov. 23:7)

Control your emotions. Don't waste your days on what you didn't enjoy or have. Just don't focus on what the devil destroys. Don't complain. It means to remain the same. You can't use human's natural thinking to win strongholds (2 Cor. 10:3–5). The devil is an imposter of thoughts. The devil will make you think it's your thought but it's his thought. You have to rebuke negative thoughts, cast it down. Stop trying to fix spiritual stuff with natural stuff. Your thoughts of doing certain things in life could be a negative thought. It might not be of God's way of thinking.

You have the power. You can have victory. Cast down fear. I can't or the word might are words having a stronghold on you. The devil is the father of lies. He never uses the word *you*. He uses the word *I*, such as *I* can't do, *I* want, or *I* might. Stick with Jesus and be everything.

Even the scripture James 2:19–20 says that the devil believes there is one God that does well. Another scripture says that faith without work is dead. We must have the right belief and put it to work. Jesus said in John 9:45, "I must work the works of him that sent me, while it is day: the night cometh when no man can work. As long as I am in the world, I am the light of the world."

If you think right, you will do right, and you will act right; and if you think wrong, you will act wrong, and you will act on things wrong. Ninety percent of the time, you will have judgment with no truth in your thoughts. People do jump to conclusions. You can't judge anything until you get the right information God called you to have.

You are blessed to do all things. If you believe you are healed, then you can be healed. You seek, you should find. If you think right, you can live right, and you will have right choices. Some of our thoughts come from how we were raised or what we were told. Some of the teachings were based on spiritual religion, and it is not just the upbringing in our homes but our churches too.

Some things are missing when told to us. Here is a thought: anything missing isn't whole. Sometimes we do feel that nothing we do is right or everything is wrong. Don't forget the devil uses the *I*, so take the *I* off of yourself. Look at the right and not the wrongs that you did. You don't have to struggle, do what you know to do. You are not stupid, you just made a mistake. You're human. Love yourself and walk in Jesus.

Give everybody the benefit of the doubt. Stop judging. Majority of the time, we don't have enough information. When you know better, you will feel better and do better. Remember, this is the day that the Lord has made, rejoice in it and be glad in it and don't be mad in it. Give everybody the benefit of the doubt. We don't know other people's situation. Stay in peace, stay calm-minded. Have patience. You know the devil will try to play you. Don't let the devil destroy your day.

A fool gets angry, the Bible says. Get the right information, get the truth. A wise man or woman will hear the matter at hand. Humble yourself, control your mouth. Do not forget that when you know better, you do better. Go repent when you are wrong. Act like a Christian. You have the power to do better. Don't judge even when others do you wrong. Pray for them, ask for forgiveness. We have the right to come to the throne. Go to God with prayer. Remember He is not mad, He is our teacher. Read in Matthew 6:9–13 the Lord's prayer.

We have more negative thoughts each day than we realize, like when we are driving. You can control your feelings, your temper. Complaining is negative, and forgiveness is a choice. God takes limits off. Bad habits? It's ours to break. You can change overnight. All you have to do is change your mind.

Everybody Comes Short

Praise God.

My subject this day is that everybody comes short. Going straight to the point, we all sin, we are born in sin.

Don't judge others!

Judgement is an expression of His chastening love for the believer. The Final Judgement is called a day of wrath for unbelievers. That is a day when believers will enter into eternal life.

We know Adam and Eve's disobedience in the garden of Eden was the beginning of sin for us. Sin is committed against three things: ourselves, others, and God. In Romans 5:12, it's saying, "Wherefore, as by one man sin entered into the world, and death by sin, and so death passed upon all men, for that all have sinned."

There is a way to get ready and be ready to enter into eternal life. We need to transform ourselves. You need to assess the new you in your spiritual life. Sinners are saved by grace, and there are two things that need to be separated: either you're dead to sin or you're going to live with God. Before, one or the other is going to take over the other. Transformation is the process of changing. You have to renew your mind and be born again. A born-again Christian is born of God and has a new DNA, which is a perfect condition, but we must continue to grow Christlike daily. Amen!

We are saved by grace, not our action. We didn't even have to work or do anything for it. It's a gift of righteousness. Righteousness is godliness that leads us to love others.

Being born in God, we have to leave the past in the past. It can stop us from growing. You need to move on and stop looking back and remembering what you went though, such as bad marriages, boyfriend, and girlfriends, relationships that weren't right for you or how your parents acted or maybe there was abuse, anger, or how you didn't like the way someone talked to you or any bad experiences or old family tradition you didn't like. Don't forget everybody comes short, but you have to remember there is no past in the new you. Let go. Don't be stuck.

Here's something to think about: when babies are born, naturally people want to see what the baby looks like, wondering who the baby favor. When you're a newborn in God, your Father God changes your image. We were born flesh of the flesh and bone of the bones.

In the Bible, Paul was a killer, but he became a born-again Christian. He had a new mindset. He said he didn't wrong anyone. Look at it this way: Jesus paid for our sin. Paul took a stand. He put the past out of his mind. Sometimes people just can't forgive, even themselves. There's nothing that God can't forgive, even the things in the past. So forgive yourself and others. Walk anew.

The devil will try to get you to think something different. He would be telling you you are not worthy, that they don't love you, or that you're just not qualified. Get free, let go. You could be stuck. You're covered under the blood. Jesus made you right. Lift up your head. You're the head and not the tail. It's not about your past or what you did. Repent. It's not about you sleeping around, on drugs, or getting pregnant out of wedlock. Just repent. Look what Jesus has done right for you. Don't look at what the people have done to you.

We all come short. You are not what you did. You're saved by grace. The mercy of God sets us free. Walk in forgiveness. You're not lacking anything because Jesus is not lacking. Look at the righteous, don't look at the wrongs. Transform yourself, live in your new DNA, and renew your mind. Start over again and stop judging yourself and others. Everybody comes short. Amen!

Walking in Love with Faith

I would like to give honor to God who is the head of my life. I just glorify and praise His holy name.

I also give honor to all of you.

First of all, I would like to say this, God is love and faith is the substance of things hoped for, the evidence of things not seen. My subject is walking in love with faith.

God knows your thoughts and He's got a plan. In Isaiah 55:8, He said,

> For my thoughts are not your thoughts nei-
> ther are your ways my ways.

Now in 1 Timothy 2:2, He said,

> All that are in authority, lead a quiet and
> peaceable life in godliness and honesty.

This means all of us because He has given us power of authority. Amen!

While walking in love, circumstances do come up. Whatever is in our heart will come out of our mouth. We must guard our mouth. We must guard our gateway, which is our mind. Thoughts will keep coming. Take power and take authority over your mind. Keep the enemy out. Guard your thoughts.

The devil can ruin you. The stronghold is in the mind. The war takes place in the mind. The stronghold pulls down negative thinking. Everything about the devil brings down your thoughts. Cast out everything that is bringing you down in the name of Jesus. Things like being selfish, self-pity, hurts, who's not in your corner will overwhelm you and cause depression. You will have no peace.

We don't have to fall down into our circumstances. Have victory. Just use all the tools God gave you. We know feelings are feelings. Don't let your feelings ruin you. The devil will go to your thoughts, your mind, but we have the mind of Christ. Go by the Word of God. Listen to the Holy Spirit. Live in the Holy Spirit. The Holy Spirit has a way to walk you through. Go to the super star, Jesus Christ. There's no need to go to an astrologist or a psychic. The more you learn about Jesus, the more you want to learn about Him. Your inner man will change.

Jesus loves people so walk in love and walk in faith. We don't have to be mean to be a Christian, telling people off, saying things like "Go to hell."

Love has patience. God doesn't write people off. God didn't write you off. Treat them with love. Here is a short testimony: there was a time I wanted to wash my hand of my sister, not knowing she really needed me. What a mistake that would have been.

We shouldn't get disappointed in people, especially those who don't go to church. Some people have seen things or have been mistreated in church. There was a time at a church when this man, a new member, didn't like to wear ties. Someone complained and told him that he needed to wear a tie, and they didn't say it in a nice way. The man and his wife were coming faithfully for about two months. They never came back after being talked to like that.

If you see or think something is wrong, pray for people who don't believe, but don't even tell them you're praying for them. A death of a loved one could be there problem. Each reacts different than the other. Motion and thoughts are involved. Most of the time, they want to get things right with the Lord. God is able to save and deliver. They may turn around and serve the Lord. He saved you and me and turned us around.

There was a time when I wanted to belong to a church. I didn't want to go back to the one I knew. I kept visiting here and there. There are others who search for a church home, just like I did. So don't stop or be scared to witness to others. You may be the one God sent to minister to them. Set an example. We need to show how to have faith in God. This is a good way to leave an inheritance to your children. Leave them with a spiritual well by showing them how to walk in faith.

Sometimes it looks worse when praying for others, it seems they're not listening to you, especially your own family. Pray for God to send someone to minister to them and for them to be delivered. We have different types of people in the world, they may be on crack, dope, or an alcoholic, people who are in a bad situation with relationships or even their health issues, but just pray.

Don't pray for God to be with you, He's already there. He will never leave you. Please don't pray to angels. God created them to be a messenger or a helper. To us, angels aren't to be identified with God, He created them. Amen!

Please don't separate yourselves from your loved ones, people in your home, your kinfolk, cousin, aunts, uncle even your grown children not living with you. They're important to Jesus.

Love your husband or wife, especially those who really don't care about what you know about Jesus. I remember a time when my husband was the one going to church and taking the children with him, asking me to go. I would stay in my bed, covering my head up and telling him a thing or two and told him to go ahead, I'm not going. I couldn't care less about church. But look at me now. God had a plan. God can reach down and turn things around. He is able and can remove the blinders off your eyes.

Don't stop walking in love with faith. Read John 3. It tells us God wants us to prosper and be in health. Walk in truth and be faithful to your brethren and strangers. He wants us to witness love on our journey. So continue walking in love with faith because there is hope by living godly and honest. Let God use His plan. His thoughts and His ways aren't ours for having a quiet and peaceful life. Amen!

The New Covenant

A Story of Easter

Jesus said "I have been very eager to eat this Passover meal with you before my sufferings begins. For I tell you now that I won't eat this meal again until its meaning is fulfilled in the Kingdom of God."

Then he took a cup of wine and gave thanks to God for it. Then He said "Take this and share it among yourselves. For I will not drink wine again until the Kingdom of God has come."

He took some bread and gave thanks to God for it. Then he broke it in pieces and gave it to the disciples saying. "This is my body which I given for you. Do this to remember me."

After supper he took another cup of wine and said "This cup is the New Covenant between God and his people—an agreement confirmed with my blood. "Which is poured out as a sacrifice for you." (Luke 22:14–20)

For I delivered unto you first of all that which I also received, how that Christ died for our sins according to the Scriptures; And that he was buried, and that he rose again the third day according to the scriptures. (1 Cor. 15:3–4)

Amen!

In the Middle

You are probably wondering, *In the middle of what?* I am speaking of your heart because in our hearts, there are issues. Issues concerning each of our lives, and our hearts should be handled with a lot of tender loving care. We can start off caring for our hearts just by listening to the Word of God. His Word is caring for us with love.

Now when we hear the Word or even see the written Word, we should store them in our hearts, right in the middle, because these words bring life into us. In other words, they are healthy for us. That is if you don't depart from them. What a good place to store them right in the middle of your heart. I'm speaking this from Proverbs 4:20–23. Amen!

We have to be responsible for our lives. What is life without love? Now in Ephesians 2:17, it's says that if we want to be like Christ, we must have Christ dwell in our hearts by faith being rooted and grounded in love. Did you know faith creates blessings? Being Christlike, we can create just like Him. He created with His words. In the beginning, God created the heaven and the earth. In the Bible, it said God said, "let there" or "let them." God called out things into existence, God blessed, just by using words.

We can create with our mouth. He even gave us power to do so. Read the book of Genesis. We need to create our life with our mouth, but we need to spend more time reading the Word and spending time with the Word. Don't you know we have the authority of all things in the name of Jesus? We even have power to speak blessings over ourselves. Why not use the power?

People, have we really realized that our blessings came verbal? God spoke His blessings. We shouldn't complain about our situation and just tell our problems to God. We should be thanking Him in the good times and the bad times. God has given us the power to change things.

I feel when we say things such as "when God sees it fit," that's giving the devil credit. We should activate our blessing, knowing you're blessed by receiving and claiming your blessing. Activate your blessing. Create with faith using the words such as "I am blessed" or "I am highly favored." Start creating with the love of God.

Don't let anyone curse your blessing, especially the devil, with negative thoughts, using word such as, "as if," "I can't," "I just can't see it," "he or she doesn't love me." Speak words knowing you are blessed right now. Amen!

Speak life. Speak healing. In the first sign of sickness, start rebuking it right then, even small things like colds, the first sniff or cough you get. Rebuke it in the name of Jesus. Healing is a choice. Jesus Christ redeemed the curses for us. We are healed by His stripes. Amen!

Satan can't get away with anything, only what we allowed him to. Knowing the things we speak, we must have faith with belief and love in the middle of our hearts.

Do not forget issues flare up in our lives. As Matthew 15:18 says, "But those things which proceed out of the mouth come forth from the heart, and they defile the man." It could be evil thoughts, such as murder, adultery, fornication, theft, false witness, and blasphemies.

It is so important to be rooted and grounded in the love of Jesus. It could make a big difference in each of our lives when there are concerns such as our finances, our children (grown or not) our marriage, for those who are single, our friends. Being rooted and grounded could make a difference in our negative and positive thoughts.

Be a creator of blessings, speak life and speak of love over one another. We know death and life is in the power of the tongue. Get more into the Word of God. Let the truth bless you with peace and joy. But most of all, put the love of Jesus in the middle of your heart. Amen!

People, there is a way in putting and not departing from the love of Jesus in the middle of our hearts, even though He has not departed from you. He is the same yesterday, today, and forever. For those who have not put God's love in the middle of their hearts or those whom departed from His love and would like to have Him in the middle of their hearts, please repeat after me:

> Heavenly Father, I come to you with the knowledge that you are God and Jesus Christ is your Son who sacrificed for my sins and was raised up from the dead and is alive. Lord, I ask that you forgive my sins, and with my heart, I ask you to be my Lord and Savior. In Jesus's name, I pray. Amen!

Now if you prayed and asked Jesus Christ into your heart as your Lord and Savior and meant it, then you need to realize that the living God, the creator of heaven and earth now lives within you. Amen!

Light the Way

Praise the Lord. I am starting this message off by saying: whosoever will.

God wants His people to make it home. He doesn't want the table to be empty. He will be disappointed if they miss out.

Not everybody will go to heaven. Not everybody will rest in peace. I say to you, go to the hedges, highway, and byways, bring others in honesty. Tell them the truth. There's still room and time. Make sure God's house isn't in need. Seek the kingdom of God. Salvation is important.

First adjust yourself by looking in the mirror. Look into your life with God. Time to save souls, but the perfect will of God is to increase His house and doing things right (Act 6:1–8). God's work must be preached and taught, and we can start in our own natural home here on earth for the increase of filling the Lord's house. God is a speaking spirit and so are we. He created by speaking, and we are God's image, a copy.

The increase needs to be in our own souls. To get that increase we, need to look in the Word, and it will teach us right. It's going to require us to work. We, as Christians, should always be ready, Always working for the King. We have to light the way for others to find their way to God.

In the book of Matthew 25, there was a wedding about to take place. In the wedding, there were ten virgins that had the responsibility to bring the lamp and oil. The lamps were torches that were made of rags and sticks. The virgins where the bride's maids. They all fell asleep waiting on the bride's groom, which was Jesus. Later during the night, they were awoken, and five of them had ran out of light, and they needed to replenish the light and wanted the other five bride's maid to share theirs, which wouldn't have been enough for all, so the five was left without light.

This story is a reminder to us that we need to stay well-lit, teachable, and always prepared. We all do get tired and weary of well-doings, but we need to hold the lamps up for others and not just throw in the towel. Have a plan, get involved. Line your plans up with God, remembering nothing from nothing leaves nothing. God wants to bless all. Talk and spend time with the ones you love. Be responsible as a child of God emotionally, financially, in health, and in business.

Remember we are the bride's maids. Get your arms ready. Stay in prayer. When you fall off-track, get back on the right road, don't be lazy. It's time to be about your Father's business. Stay on the right road. God sees your heart. He knows your desire. Keep working at it. Don't exit, don't quit. God will strengthen you, just seek God. God knows we need rest. Being tired isn't a sin. Remember, light attracts attention. There will come a time when it will be too late. Walk in love. We are the light of the world. Never let your oil burn out (Lev. 6:13). Amen!

LOVE

Giving honor to whom honor is due and that is my Lord Savior.

My subject is love. How can you walk in it if you haven't learned about it? How are you going to know love? We have to learn to receive the love.

How do we come in the knowledge of love? The lack of not knowing our relationship with God leads to us not knowing how to love God (the book Hosea). When learning the love of God, we accept by faith not because we got to. We humble our hearts. "We love Him because He first loved us" (1 John 4:19). If we reject it, we will reject Him. We're accepted by God based on His grace, respect, and honor. Perfect love means believing and accepting God's love. Perfect love casts out all fear. Fear brings torment. Your flesh and mind will always bring in the enemy of fear.

Walking in the love of God when we get hurt is like having a hole in our hearts. "He restoreth my soul" (Ps. 23). Emotion is your soul, it's your mind. What is the hole in your heart? It's the lack of knowledge. We have to let God take over our inner man.

When healing a broken heart, knowledge brings power and confidence. We really don't know the ins and outs of love. Relationships help us use natural things, such as marriage. Marriage is one of the most important decision you make that help us understand love and the love of God.

Do we really need to know the Principle of Love? "To be ready for marriage." You don't need to have a test before marriage like a driver's test. Many people will break their marriage just like a car could be broken-down by parts. When trust breaks down, the relationship breaks up. We need to receive knowledge. Relationship is not about choosing the right person, it's about you. Marriage is not a commandment. You don't have to have a partner to be happy. Love doesn't keep two people together; wisdom is the principal thing (Prov. 4:7–8). Get wisdom, get understanding. Nothing is more important than love.

Talking about Christians, we can't be a know-it-all. Talking isn't listening. When you know better, you will do better. You can't teach if you don't know how to be a student of the Word. Love has to be in you. Love is not a feeling, it's a choice. The more you learn to love, the more love you will have. Love is understanding the value. Love can be measured; it can be paid. Jesus paid for our love.

People are priceless; we value our worth. It is the price Jesus paid for us, redeemed for us. If people only knew what value our life is, something we ourselves don't know yet.

We're made of the image and likeness of God. God is love. We're made in love. Next to air, we need love. We were made out of love, by love. Love is an act of our will (St. John 13: 34–35, Rom. 13:8).

Being born again means you're a spirit. The spirit and soul live on in the eternal. The body will drop out. Get your spirit right and get born again. Your soul needs to get saved when it gets beat up. The mind is soul, its feelings and thinking. Spirit it is intact. Spirit and soul have to be lined up with the mind. I can do things though Christ which strengthen me (Phil. 4–13). The spirit changes, not the soul changes. The only medicine that can heal the soul is the Word of God (Luke 4:18). Amen!

After Thanksgiving Day

Praise the Lord, everyone. God is Good!

I am very thankful for all He has done for me through all the years of my life. How about you? I thank Him for traveling mercy this day and for all the things He has provided when I was in need. He is an on-time God. He is just a good God. Amen!

I shall continue to have praises in my heart. He knows our hearts, and I thank Him that the blood still works. *Amen!*

Jesus loves people, all types of people (John 3). It tells us God wants us to prosper and be in health. Walk in truth, do faithfully to your brethren and strangers. He wants us to witness love on our journey. Let God use His plans. His thoughts and ways aren't ours in having a quiet peaceful life. Here is a quote; I read, you can't keep it unless you give it away having to receive healing and spiritual renewal, we retain them, only as we offer to help others. This quote is used as a viewpoint showing the difference between recovering programs and the Christian churches. Holy Spirit will always give you the right answer, but you must respond right. There is a scripture that talks about when we enter into our closet and shut the door. How can we shut the door when things keep falling out? We haven't picked up, cleaned up, or cleared out some things. Have we realized how blessed we are when God has already spoken His blessings over us? I am thankful always, in the good or the bad times.

Learn to forgive yourself; forgiveness is power. When praying forgive others as well. In Ephesians 4:32, it says to be kind to one another. (Eph. 4:29) Let no corrupt communication proceed out of your mouth.

In Philippians 4:5–7, it says,

> (5) Let your moderation be known to all men. The Lord is at hand.
>
> (6) Be careful of nothing; but in everything by prayer and supplication with thanksgiving let your requests be made known to God.
>
> (7) And the peace of God, which passeth all understanding. Shall keep your hearts and mind through, Christ Jesus.

Here, it's speaking of your gentleness and saying to not be anxious. Ask for something humbly or make a humble request. Here, we know He wants us to understand as we go through problems in our health, money, home, job, dreams, and other situation.

God is God of blessing, full of joy and peace. You will feel His presence. Trust in God. God gives double for our troubles. And His mercy is new every day. Don't drift away from God or you won't be able to hear His voice. Be careful, don't let things slip. Life is too short. Repent when it is needed. Do something meaningful in your life. Show others how blessed you are. Tell your testimony on how God has been good to you. Tell about His mercy and His grace. We all know His mercy is His blessing. Be grateful by showing action. We know grace is the love and favor of God toward human beings.

We are saved by grace, not by our actions. We didn't even have to work or do anything for it. It's a gift of righteousness. Righteousness is godliness and that means for us to love one another. The Bible is a love letter. God is love and the Word is God, and the Word is truth. Don't let your heart be troubled. Sometimes we feel we're all alone. Remember you're not alone, you have the favor of God. What is life without love? Ephesians 2:17 says if we want to be like Christ, we must have Christ dwell in our hearts by faith, rooted and grounded in love.

Put the love of Jesus in the middle of your heart. He is the same yesterday, today, and forever. Amen!

THE BENEFITS GAINED BY THE BELIEVERS FROM CHRIST SUFFERING

Think about how Christ suffered for us. I'm thinking about all the mumbling and grumbling about things of the flesh, natural things of the body, such as headache, backache, earache. The little lite rope or string burn, I have had. Not forgetting the weather side of it. Complaining about it's too hot or too cold. As a woman the blood I lost with a little cut or being on my menstrual, isn't nothing compared to the blood Christ poured out for me. The word *Nafesh* means "life in the blood" (Lev. 17:11).

I am thankful for all the benefits I've received from Christ. He suffered for me, and I truly say THANK YOU, JESUS! I am blessed to have a mind to think with, eyes to see with, hands to feel with, and feet to stand on. There is no comparison when standing in line, receiving things or carrying things that seem too heavy. There isn't any comparison receiving disturbing thoughts in my mind and heart that's too heavy to handle, which I probably shouldn't have accepted in the first place. During the good times or bad times of my life, there is no comparing to how, (Matt. 27:29–30) Christ had the cross on His back, falling and getting pushed around or spit on. I feel this has happened to me at times.

Christ reminds me of the love we have for our family, how a mother and father should be loving toward their children, and how children should be loving and respectful toward their parents, just like Jesus loves and respects His Father God. As we know, "Honor Your Father and Mother" (Exod. 20:12)

I am blessed to be part of the body of Christ, a Christian family. How all of us as come to love one another as it should always be

(Luke 10:27)? I have more trust and faith (1 Col.2:5) in Jesus who is the (Abba) Father, the head of my life (Col.1:14–18), not forgetting to have more patience and understanding toward others. Christ has been thorough all the tears, sweat, heartaches, and betrayal I thought I have had (Col 12:2). My tears, sweat, heartaches, and betrayal is nothing compared to what Jesus has gone through with all these things for me. (Cor. 11:23).

The thought of who's going to give me the last glass of water or where will my next meal come from, especially at times when I feel down with low self-esteem or feeling like I have done so much for others, is a very foolish thought when I know Jesus has suffered so much for me to have water and food (Matt. 6:25). I know it doesn't take silver, gold, or money, as people say, to have a friend like Jesus in my life. I have gained more benefits than most with Jesus in my life than I have without (Exod. 20:22–23). I have a trusting friend to pray with, talk with, walk with, eat with, sleep with, and wake me up each day with the spirit of love in my heart (Rom. 5:5). *I, again, say thank you, Jesus,* for all the benefits I have gained through *you* (Ps. 103).

Thanks to the Lord for Change

This is the psalm of praise where David expressed his thanks to the Lord for the changes in his life. When I have such a praise in my heart, I know He has changed me. I thank Him always for the changes in my life. My attitude is one of the things that has been changed, like the stubbornness I had in my heart. Most of the time, it was my way or the highway. Which this kind of attitude got me in trouble, it kept me from not listening to others or just being disobedient at other times.

David was a person who had an unduly high opinion of himself. He was haughty and arrogant. He was one who was satisfied in something that he had done. He had a lot of pride in himself, but some things just weren't right in is heart. No matter what, his heart was with God.

Here is where God is different. He only has a momentary anger, and He is slow to anger (Nah. 1:3). Wrath means having a strong anger. Human wrath may kindle by false accusation or disobedience, but God's wrath is excised against ungodliness, idolatry, and unbelief. He is such a merciful God, so compassionate. We all should be followers of the Lord, with forgiveness in our hearts.

In this Psalms David is thanking the Lord for healing him. I know I am so grateful for the healing the Lord has brought into my life. I have been healed from a heart attack, also I have been healed from cancer. I am just so thankful. These are the times when I felt this was the end of my life, but in going through, it taught me how to have faith in the Lord. I know in my heart He is the true healer. He has healed me from many illnesses in my lifetime.

Like David, give thanks. God is good. Sometimes it seems so dark in our life it feels like our back is up against a wall. Not able to get out of that dark place. Sometimes it has something to do with our living condition such as our finance needs or health. Not just our own needs, it could be someone else needs, that you feel there's nothing you can do to help. But with the goodness of the Lord, things can change.

We all go through things most of the time. At these times, it helps us just to get closer to our Lord and Savior. He wants a relationship with each of us. We might not feel close to God, but we must remember salvation cannot be earned, it is a gift of God's grace (Eph. 2:8). It's God's unmerited favor and love which leads Him to grant salvation to believers through the exercise of their faith in Jesus Christ. Though faith in Christ, God's righteousness is imputed or granted to believers (Titus 3:5).

Psalms 30 has me thinking of the goodness of the Lord which is part of the fruit of the spirit which should be characterized by followers of Christ. It means purity and righteousness. True goodness comes from God who is holy, righteous, merciful, and loving. Not forgetting holiness is moral purity to be set apart and sanctified for service to God. God is holy (Exod. 15:11) and He expects holiness of people (Rom. 12:1). Godliness is holy living and righteous behavior which issues from devotion to God. Godliness also leads to love for others.

As I was saying earlier, we all go through things. That's when it seems like we are in such a dark place in our lives. We could be crying, worrying, and wondering what is going to happen next. There are times when, like David, we beg God for His mercy. We pray, "Lord, help me. I don't know what to do," or "Lord, show me the way." He hears our humble cries. We need to be still and listen to God on what He is telling us to do at these times. We, at times, just want to try things our way, being stubborn just like David or being too arrogant, thinking our way is the best way of doing things.

God disciplines His children through corrective actions. He trains or teaches us like our natural parents here on earth do. "Impart important truths to a child" (Prov. 22:6). A disciplined person also controls his impulses, speech, and action. He sees when his chastisement is at work and when it worked. If only we all let God be God. He can change everything.

There is nothing like crying or weeping and waking up with joy on your heart. His gift of mercy is so abundant and fresh every morning. God has a gentle and steadfast love and mercy which He extends freely to all. The Lord is such a good God. He gives us chances after chances to get things right. He's just a forgiving God. He forgives the things we mess up in our lives. We all need to learn forgiveness and love, just like what the Lord is trying to teach each us.

Another thing that comes to mind when reading Psalms 30 is hope. People give up so easily, especially when they have to do things the hard way or take the long way. This is part of the test the Lord has given us, and we also need to remember that hope is a sure and steady faith in God's promises. We, as believers, have to have hope in God's promise of salvation, resurrection, and eternal life.

God healed David and forgave his sin. Just like David, I have praises for the Lord in my heart always. He heals me, forgives me, and He chastises me from time to time. The Lord has made so many changes in my life that even deep down in my heart, He has changed my way of thinking. I am so happy to serve the Lord.

Not just for David and me, His love is for everyone. I give the Lord honor and all high praises. Hallelujah!

Suggested Scripture
for Daily Living

Psalms 91

(1) He that dwelleth in the secret place of the most High shall abide under the shadow of the Almighty.

(2) I will say of the Lord, He is my refuge and my fortress: my God; in him will I trust.

(3) Surely he shall deliver thee form the snare of the fowler, and from the noisome pestilence.

(4) He shall cover thee with his feathers, and under his wings shalt thou trust: his truth shall be thy shield and buckler.

(5) thou shalt not be afraid for the terror by night: nor fir the arrow the flieth by day;

(6) Nor fir the pestilence that walketh in darkness; nor for the destruction that wasteth at noonday.

(7) A thousand shall fall at thy side, and ten thousand at thy right hand; but it shall not come nigh thee.

(8) Only with tine eyes shalt thou behold and see the reward of the wicked.

(9) because thou hast made the Lord, which is my refuge, even the most High, thy habitation;

(10) there shall no evil befall thee, neither shall any plague come nigh thy dwelling.

(11) For he shall give his angels charge over, to keep thee in all thy ways.

(12) they shall bear thee up in their hands, lest thou dash thy foot against a stone.

(13) thou shalt tread upon the lion and adder: the young lion and the dragon shalt thou trample under feet.

(14) Because he hath set his love upon me, there will I deliver him: I will set him on high, because he hath known my name.

(15) He shall call upon me, and I will answer him: I will be with him, and honour him.

(16) With long life will I satisfy him, and shew him my salvation.

Psalms 23

The Lord is my shepherd; I shall not want.

He maketh me to lie down in green pastures: he leadeth me beside the still waters.

He restoreth my soul: he leadeth me in the paths of righteousness for his name's sake.

Yeas, though I walk through the valley of the shadow of death. I will fear no evil: for thou art with me; thy rod and thy staff they comfort me.

Thou prepares a table before me in the presence of mine enemies: thou anoinest my head with oil; my cup runneth over.

Surely goodness and mercy shall follow me all the days of my life: and I will dwell in the house of the Lord forever.

Psalm 103

Bless the Lord, O my soul; and all that is within me bless his holy name.

Bless the Lord, O my soul and forget not all his benefits:

Who forgiveth all thine iniquities; who healeth all thy diseases;

Who redeemeth thy life from destruction; who crowneth thee with lovingkindness and tender mercies:

Who satisfieth thy mouth with good things; so that thy youth is renewed like the eagle's.

The Lord executeth righteousness and judgement for all that are oppressed.

He made known his ways unto Moses, his acts unto the children of Israel.

The Lord is merciful and gracious, slow to anger, and plenteous in mercy.

He will not always chide: neither will he keep his anger forever.

He hath not dealt with us after our sins; nor rewarded us according to our iniquities.

For as the heaven is high above the earth, so great is his mercy toward them that fear him.

As far as the east is from the west, so far hath he removed our transgressions from us.

Like as a father pitieth his children, so the Lord pitieth them that fear him.

For he knoweth our frame; he remembereth that we are dust.

As for man, his days are as grass: as a flower of the field, so he flourisheth.

For the wind passeth over it, and it is gone; and the place there-of shall know it no more.

But the mercy of the Lord is from everlasting to everlasting upon them that fear him, and his righteousness unto children's children;

To such as keep his covenant, and to those that remember his commandments to do them.

The Lord hath prepared his throne in the heavens; and his kingdom ruleth over all.

Bless the Lord, ye his angels, the excel in strength, that do his commandments, hearkening unto the voice of his word.

Bless ye the Lord, all ye his hosts; ye ministers of his, that do his pleasure.

Bless the Lord, all his works in all places of his dominion: bless the Lord, O my soul.

Prayer for Salvation

Heavenly Father, I come to You in the Name of Your Son Jesus Christ. You said in Your word that whosoever shall call upon the name of the Lord shall be saved (Romans 10:13). I am calling on Jesus right now. I believe He died on the cross for my sins, that He was raised from the dead on the third day. Lord Jesus, I am asking You now, come into my heart. Take control of my life and help me be what You want me to be. I repent of my sins and surrender myself totally and completely to You. I accept You and confess You as my Lord and Savior. Thank you for making me a new person and forgiving me.

Epilogue

To everyone who has read *Spoken and Unspoken Messages*, I say to you out of faith, hope, and love, I feel we, as Christian, should let our light shine bright so we can help others find their bright light. That bright light is the shining star, our Lord Savior.

Remember, the Lord wants to reach everyone with His messages. He sends different messengers and uses different methods of giving His messages. His messages stay the same. It never changes no matter where it is coming from. We need to celebrate, praise, and thank God for all He has done.

We can't put the Holy Spirit in a box. We need to stay well lit. Be teachable and always be prepared. We do get tired and weary of well-doings, but being regenerated helps believers overcome the world and lead a victorious life. We need to hold the lamps up for others and not just throw in the towel. Don't forget that light attracts attention and being tired isn't a sin.

Sometimes we feel we're all alone, but remember, you're not alone, you have favor of God. Tell people about the good news, and that is: Jesus paid the price for us and our sin. Nothing shall separate us. He will help strengthen with the abilities. Just keep loving God and people. Without love, we are nothing. So I say to you, walk in love. We are the light of the world. So never let your oil burn out.

With all my faith, hope, and love to you,

Dr. Diane Cross

Resources

The Holy Bible
The Old and New Testaments
Authorized King James Version
Thomas Nelson Bible
A Division of Thomas Nelson, Inc.

Bible Dictionary
George W. Knight and Rayburn W. Ray

Webster's New Dictionary
Form the Editors of Western's New World Dictionary

ABOUT THE AUTHOR

Rev. Dr. Diane Cross gives God all praises, honor, and the glory for He is worthy of all.

She is a widow. She is a past girlfriend and lover for forty-eight years to the same man, Arnold Cross. She is a mother of three sons, grandmother, and a great-grandmother. All is such a joy in her life.

She dedicates her life to the Lord. She gives Him all praise, honor, and glory that is due to Him all because He is worthy of all. She is the author of another book called *My Dot to Dot Connection*, which is her autobiography.

She has a doctor's degree in theology. She is also known as Reverend, Chaplain, and a Certified Community Emergency Rescue Team (CERT). She has been a Sunday school teacher to many, young and old. Others call her Mom, Grandma, Sis, Doc. Ladydi, all with love and kindness.

She loves to greet and meet people with love and kindness as well. She prays that this book will help each of you some way, somehow in your daily walk of life.

9 781098 030889